# Angels &
# DRAGONS

# MOLLY WOLF

DOUBLEDAY  *New York London Toronto Sydney Auckland*

# Angels & DRAGONS

ON SORROW, GOD AND HEALING

PUBLISHED BY DOUBLEDAY
a division of Random House, Inc.
1540 Broadway, New York, New York 10036

DOUBLEDAY and the portrayal of an anchor with a dolphin are
trademarks of Doubleday, a division of Random House, Inc.

Book design by Bonni Leon-Berman

"For a Sad Lady" by Dorothy Parker used by kind permission of
Penguin Putnam Inc. (U.S.) and Gerald Duckworth & Co Ltd (U.K.).
Quote from "It Don't Bring You" by Mary Chapin Carpenter used by
kind permission of Hal Leonard Corporation.

Library of Congress Cataloging-in-Publication Data
Wolf, Molly, 1949–
    Angels & dragons: on sorrow, God and healing / Molly Wolf.— 1st ed.
        p. cm.
    1. Meditations.    I. Title: Angels and dragons.    II. Title.
    BV4832.3 .W65 2001
    242—dc21                        2001028171

ISBN 0-385-50122-6

Printed in the United States of America
November 2001
First Edition
10   9   8   7   6   5   4   3   2   1

# CONTENTS

# CONTENTS

## Part Three
## In the Mouth of the Lion

## Part Four
## Wrestling Angels

# Preface

"A collection of vignettes drawn from life, inter-
spersed with meditations on where theology intersects with real
life." That's what my book contract said and that's what the pub-
lisher wanted. It sounded easy enough. I've been writing for years
about where theology intersects with real life; that's my vocation,
and also my delight. I trawl my way through life looking for places
where I can find God at work, and since God is all over the map,
I rarely have any problems.

But this book (my editor said) was to be a little different. This
time, he wanted me to trawl not through my surroundings, but
through my own history. Go back (he told me) and pick out

places in your own life where God has been, and write about those. Okay, I said. I guess I can do that. So I treated myself to a second-hand IBM ThinkPad, turned on the memory tapes, and settled down to produce a book, as specified.

You probably know the apocryphal Chinese curse, "May you live in Interesting Times." My times have, on the whole, been Interesting, sometimes very Interesting, although not in grand and dramatic ways. On a real level, my life has been about as eventful as a typical Jane Austen novel. But it's also been packed, in a quiet way, with Big Emotional Stuff—loss, abuse, emotional trauma, survival, and (now increasingly) redemption, faith, change, healing.

As I trawled through my past, trying to find things to write about, the memories surfaced. Often they were painful. Sometimes the pain was blooming, like a big red Georgia O'Keeffe poppy; sometimes it was sharper, like a bad back molar. Sometimes it grumbled away like a deep sciatic ache. Each essay had to be ground out the very hard way—and normally I find writing so easy that the effort itself was a shock. Moreover, as I wrote, another sort of pain emerged. I have post-traumatic stress disorder; it had been latent when I started writing, but as the memories surfaced, so did the PTSD. I wrote it all out, one piece at a time.

But as I wrestled with each chunk of pain or PTSD, I turned on it the light of my faith: where is God in all this? What's the meaning here? How can I make sense of this in light of my Christian beliefs? It's not enough for me simply to experience and report on my experience: I am driven to meld my life and my belief into one unpartable whole, "as my two eyes make one in sight." What does the driving? Some sort of inner sense of rightness, of integrity: This is as it should be. I am God's critter and have known that since I was a child of nine (even if I forgot for a while). I have come to accept that fact with a sense of deep relief, and I let God do the driving a lot—or so I hope.

So this is a book of dragons and angels: of pain and healing, of the darkness of loss and the light of redemption. Some of the pieces wanted to be essays and others wanted to be stories, and I gave each piece its head and wrote it as it wanted to be written. Once the pieces were all done, I did what any essayist does: I laid them all out and saw how they wanted to be arranged. Arranging them was easy enough, but then I thought of trying to link them into some sort of coherent narrative. That wouldn't happen. You're holding a book of individual pieces; perhaps you can construct a structured, thematic narrative from them, but I can't. I hope that's all right with you.

Thanks to Trace Murphy, my editor, who did significant handholding throughout the process; thanks to my wonderful agent, Linda Roghaar, and to all who were involved in the book's production. Thanks to Henry, Ross, and John for putting up with me while I was writing. Thanks to Lyn Williams Keeler, who has worked with me on trauma issues for the last three years. Thanks to Jane and Eileen, Anne, Connie, Beth, my dollink Debele, Bill the Blyster, and all others who read chunks of the book and told me it really wasn't nearly as gawdawfulhorriblenobloodygood as I thought it was. Bless you all.

This book is for my mother and personal theological trainer, Barbara Wolf, who walked me through every single step of this journey. Much love, Ma.

*"Serpents can grow wings to become dragons, and dragons can be tamed to become simultaneously fierce and gentle servants of God."*

M. SCOTT PECK

# *Part One*

# THE SCREEN HOUSE

## *A Collection of Things*

I am sitting out here in my screen house, a twelve-by-twelve-by-seven gray-and-green business of cheap tent fabric and screens, poles and zippers. It is early summer. I can hear the guys across the creek playing softball or soccer—either's likely enough around here. The neighbor's dog barks whenever it occurs to her, which is often, but it's warm enough that she settles down quickly. There's the soft sound of cars on the road, the temporary boom of someone's oversized car radio. Down the street somewhere a mother calls to her kids in the backyard. These small, normal sounds don't break the silence within; they only enforce it.

This screen house. I got it as a treat for myself, a private place where I could be away from the phone and kids' squabbles and housework and constant mini-crises. We first tried to set it up a couple of months ago; it takes all four of us, me, my guy, and my two sons, to put the thing up. I'm good with tents and similar structures, but this thing is a truly outstandingly lousy piece of design. The first time we put it up, it fell down within an hour or so. Then the skies opened and it rained for three weeks, and other things came up, so the screen house lay out on the grass, propped against the rotting picnic table, for more than a month. Second try: the guys and I shook the water out of the plastic folds and put the screen house up again. As we tried to brace the roof up, a slug fell on my older kid's arm, and he was totally grossed out. This time the thing stayed up for, oh, must have been five or six hours. Then it fell down again. And it rained again, this time for almost five weeks, without hardly a break. It's been the wettest spring anyone can remember.

But then the weather broke, and I rustled the guys outside, groaning, elder son pointedly remembering the slug, and we shook the water out of the plastic folds yet again and hoisted the poles—three arches, one in the center and one at each end—and lifted the wet, grass-stained, dirty folds. Those stains may or may not ever come out. The guys held the poles up while I frantically pegged the base down and punched holes in the dirt for the pole ends to sit in, so that they couldn't slide around. Even with all that, the tent was terribly shaky; it was a fairly windy day, and the thing swayed like a vertiginous drunk. So I took yellow polypropylene rope, and I strapped the northwest corner of the screen house to our conveniently located westernmost spruce tree, and the northeast corner to another spruce tree, and I took a couple of spare poles and braced the southern corners, guying the braces strongly in place. That did the trick. Those trees aren't going anywhere.

Now I sit in my screen house listening to the gentle flapping of cheap tent fabric, but knowing it's not going to fall down. Even when it's hit by a strong gust, the fabric shudders and rustles, but the frame stays solid. The screen house, which cannot stand on its own even in a mild breeze, is now strongly tied to something big and rooted, and it's just fine. I sit here at a plastic table with a Coleman lamp on it (so that I can come out here to read at night), and the mosquitoes haven't figured out how to get in (at least not yet, not many), and my back field ripples greenly as the wind passes over it.

I too will always need to be tethered to something strong and deep-rooted, something that's not going anywhere. "I leaned my back against an oak," the song says, "thinking it was a trusty tree. / But first it bent and then it broke / and so did my false love to me." There is only the one love that will not, sooner or later, prove false, because humans are only human. And that love is Love.

My screen house sits at the top of my backyard, which slopes downward a couple of hundred feet to the creek at the back. The top of the yard is reasonably civilized by rural standards, if not by suburban ones; it's mostly grass—weedy, lumpy, ill-trimmed grass, but grass. We have an ongoing battle with brambles and burdocks that sway back and forth each year. I'm winning this year, whacking the brambles down with an electric hedge trimmer—take that, you sucker, woo!—but there's no completely defeating them. The wild things, on the other hand, securely own the field below the low stone wall that separates front from back. The field hasn't been mowed for at least five or six years; one large Manitoba maple (a fast-growing weed tree) now dominates it, and there's a tangle of wild grape growing up the wall, behind which we put all our yard litter, leaves and pruned stuff. My cats know this territory; to them, it's probably as familiar as my house itself. But I don't know it. I don't even go there most years. I don't need to.

I used to want to know EVERYTHING about the things I was interested in: because I wanted to know why a cream puff puffs, I started taking food science courses, and they led me into biology and biochemistry and microbiology and all sorts of stuff, most of which has long since departed my brain because it's strictly "use it or lose it." Learning is, I believe, about as much fun as a person can have with her clothes on. But I have learned to live in a comforting awareness of my ignorance of my yard.

I know that it's full of micro-communities. Insects and field mice live and breed and die in the tangle of wild grape; there are plant communities, competing perhaps, or maybe cooperating, but certainly interacting as living systems always do. Because of those biology and biochemistry courses, I am acutely aware of the great natural gyres of water, carbon, oxygen, hydrogen, magnesium, that my yard is a tiny part of: plants uptaking carbon dioxide, stripping off the oxygen and releasing it, gluing the carbons into simple sugars, assembling the sugars into complex chains that form the plant's tissues; the enormous constant wheeling of water through the system, rain, dew, snow, slush, water vapor, the creek down at the back, the river system it flows into. My screen house is practically on top of our septic tank, and I have a pretty fair idea of what's happening there too. That water too has spent time in the sea and in other living bodies before passing into, through, and out of my own.

Regarding this natural world with sappy sentimentality is insulting it, and seeing it as cruelly competitive is reading into it things that don't belong to it. Cruelty requires intent, and living things don't operate intentionally; only we do that. The people I know who *do* know what's going on in my backyard, expertly and in detail, see it as being neither sweet nor grim but simply marvelous—full of wonders, from the incredible numbers of the tiny land snails in the dry drift down by the creek to the mass and majesty of the big maples out front. They do bioblitzes, counting every single living thing in a given area of land, a complete inventory. I admire them greatly. But I admire God more greatly for knowing about all the land snails that the field biologists didn't find, all the Manitoba maple seeds that got away.

I know how little I *do* know about what goes on in my backyard, what events govern the field mice's lives, what the ground hogs are up to. And this is comforting, because it means I don't *have* to know everything. Because I am aware of my ignorance in-stead of cherishing it blindly, it keeps me comfortably human. I don't have all the answers, and that's as it should be.

*C*_gust of wind snaps a sheet on the line, and I jump—I startle very easily—at the sudden *crack!* This morning, under a dark blue sky, I hung out a couple of loads, feeding the mama mosquitoes and listening to a group of crows play-fight like teenagers through my trees and the trees next door. I have just been reading Kathleen Norris's *The Quotidian Mysteries: Laundry, Liturgy and "Women's Work,"* and I am glad to see that somebody else appreciates the spiritual richness of laundry.

> *It is precisely these thankless, boring, repetitive tasks that are hardest for the workaholic or utilitarian mind to appreciate, [but] God knows that being rendered temporarily mindless as we toil is what allows us to ap-proach the temple of holy leisure. When confronting a sinkful of dirty dishes—something I do regularly, as my husband is the cook in our house and I am the dishwasher—I admit that I generally lose sight of the fact that God is inviting me to play.* *

Hanging out the laundry, like cooking or doing dishes, per-mits me to slip into that state where I am actively contemplative,

*Kathleen Norris, *The Quotidian Mysteries: Laundry, Liturgy and "Women's Work"* (New York: Paulist Press, 1998), p. 27.

something that's invaluable for a writer and a Christian. I think it's because the work gives my body and senses something simple to play with, something that doesn't need my active involvement, so that my soul can be free to wander and worship. Think of a mother giving her children crayons and paper in church, so that they could settle down quietly and draw, sitting on the kneeler and using the pew as a desk, and she herself could withdraw at least a little of her attention from them and listen to the sermon. And so I've learned to cherish this Martha-work. Sometimes it's just a drag, and I'm grateful for help, but sometimes I almost resent it when my husband wants to "take some of the load" to spare me. I don't want to be spared. This is when I slip away and get to be at least a little closer to God, which is where I most definitely want to be.

I think I would go a step further than Norris and ask if workaholism and utilitarianism are both disordered states, while meditative work at its best is aligned with the Spirit and flowing happily in that direction—at least when it's going as it should be, not as it so frequently does.

I remember once being told by a very old man that in the old days, when you still sawed wood and churned butter and reaped hay and split firewood by hand instead of by machinery, you worked at a steady rate: one stroke per second, sixty strokes a minute. No faster, no slower. If you tried to go faster, you'd only exhaust yourself, and slow wouldn't get the job done. That's wise. I don't hustle to get the laundry out, because that would center me on my haste and worry, not on my prayer; but neither do I slack and spend a few minutes staring out over the backyard to the creek. It's the rhythm. Sixty strokes per minute. God, that is as much as I can manage sometimes; but you know that already.

Workaholism/utilitarianism are to work as materialism/casual destructiveness are toward things: either a destructive overvaluing or a destructive undervaluing of God-given stuff that we should value in a balanced, healthy way. We shouldn't be driven about work and material things, and we shouldn't be casually contemptuous of them either. For they too are incarnational, part of *this* life that we're supposed to live as fully as we possibly can, neither clinging to it nor dismissing it.

This life isn't something we're supposed to grapple desperately on to, as though there's nothing else that matters; nor is it something we're supposed to get through as quickly, inattentively, and contemptuously as we can because it's not what *really* matters. We are incarnate for damned good reasons, body and spirit shaping each other. We're starting to learn what strong, subtle, and permanent scars a hurt spirit can leave on the body's patterns; we have no idea how important the body is in shaping the spirit. I can use these terms, these oppositions, but they're false. In this life, my body and spirit are one and the same. In the next life—well, I'll figure that out when I get there, in God's good time.

For the time being, this Martha-work is one of the ways in which the whole of me, body and soul, somehow pulls together, fully and happily at one for the glory of God—at least sometimes, and that will do.

In another hour or so, the laundry will be mostly dry, except for the heavy stuff. I'll zip myself out of the screen house, collect my denim sundress off the line while it's still slightly damp, and take it inside to be ironed with its two sister dresses and some shirts. And ironing will be a sort-of prayer, although not a prayer that I could verbalize or you could overhear. More a floating of the soul Godward while my hands do what they've been doing for years and will do for years to come. Martha-work: invaluable.

When I started a minute ago at the flapping of that sheet, I jarred the plastic table that my laptop sits on, and my fountain pen rolled off and dropped into the grass. I love this pen, a cheap but friendly Schaeffer, because whenever I think I've lost it (I lose things easily), it comes back, reappearing in a notebook or the bottom of my purse as if by magic. It feels almost as though it's destined to come back to my hand, whatever happens. Now I lean down to scoop it up. As I sit up again, my cross bangs gently against my chest, calling for attention, perhaps. (Oh, I know it's really only inertia and gravity, but can't we be imaginative here?)

I slipped the heavy silver chain around my neck this morning, first thing, as I do most mornings, automatically. I did a bit of praying when I woke up because I find that a satisfying thing to do (and something that needs to be done even when it's not satisfying). As always, the chain was cold on my skin for a moment, and then the two of us settled down to an almost unconscious companionable co-journeying.

I have worn this cross for almost five years now, the longest any cross and I have kept company together, and I expect to wear it for years to come. Like my fountain pens, it seems to be one of the very rare items that I apparently *can't* lose. I came across it in one of those moments that any half-decent psychologist could have a field day with. A month or so after the end of my long, abusive marriage, I redid my bedroom—stripped up the horrible carpet, fixed up the cracks in the ceiling, patched the big hole where he'd put his fist through the wallboard, thrown out the old bed and the shabby curtains—and painted the room a quiet grayish green with ivory trim. And in the course of these renovations, I found a trinket box, put on a high shelf way back in the closet. I'd completely forgotten about the box; I'd bought it twenty-five years before, and it held all sorts of small treasures that I'd lost all remembrance of— my charm bracelet from high school, a locket on a long silver chain, this cross, which my mother had bought for my father and my father (it wasn't to his taste) had given to me. I took the chain from the locket and slung the cross on it, and now we spend our days together, it and I.

It's a big, heavyish thing, almost two inches long and an inch and a quarter across, solid silver. It is a classic Celtic cross, with a circle uniting the four arms, and at the center a child holding what seems to be an ax or mallet, or perhaps a lily; it's too small to tell. On the arms are crammed all sorts of tiny scenes and elements: a harper, a flutist, an armed man with a large shield, two shepherds with a pair of sheep, two figures talking to each other, two figures embracing, and a couple of graceful Celtic whirligigs, very handsome. Bluntly, I haven't got a clue what these all mean, although I suppose the harpist is probably David and the embracing figures could be the Prodigal Son and his father. That they all do have some meaning I don't doubt for a second. They are so clearly symbols. If I knew the maker, I could ask, and he or she could tell me what all these figures and elements are, and then I would know the summed-up meaning of this particular cross.

I have spent six struggling costive months or so writing about my own figures and elements, scenes from a life. Looking over what I have written, I'm not sure what the overall meaning is—except that I am like my screen house: unless I'm firmly tied to God, I don't stand up at all well, especially in any sort of wind. I know that my catalogue of scenes is anything but complete, in part because I figure much of this stuff would probably bore you to tears and in part because I know there's a whole lot I don't remember at all. The shape and pattern of my life, like my cross, is something I can learn only from my Maker. I will probably not be able to ask him about it until I'm on face-to-face terms with the one "who formed me in my mother's womb."

Again, knowing that I don't know is obscurely comforting. I would as soon be like the psalmist lying peacefully back in Abba's arms, like a toddler on his mother's lap. (But I also know that, like a toddler, I would insist on wriggling free and skittering off at high speed, bent on exploring.) What I do know is this: I will entrust God with my past; certainly he can make more sense of it than I can.

*I* said that I startle easily and that I have problems with memory: I've lost some times, I know that, and other times come back to me with all the emotional life and color wiped out of them; or the color comes back (mostly dark stuff, grief, anger, self-eating) with no obvious form or outline. When it's bad, my breathing gets tight and shallow as anxiety squeezes my ribs together and I rub my sternum, trying to get easement. Or I find myself wrapping my arms about myself, head down, shoulders rounded and clenched. When it's bad, I go floating away, absolutely elsewhere, and reality narrows to something quite shrunken and vivid, as though my whole focus had gone wonky. When it's bad, I have no emotions when emotions ought to be flying around like startled bats; but I have memories that drift across my vision, wraithlike: memories of the violence. Or else I am seized and shaken by emotions that I don't understand: mostly pain, a lot of anger, bubbling up slowly like boiling chocolate pudding. When it's bad, my family knows that Mum's a little crazy again.

I have post-traumatic stress disorder, the result of a long, crazy, and sometimes violent marriage, an Alice-in-Wonderland world in which the unspoken line—because not-speaking this stuff is a big part of it—was *I didn't do anything wrong and besides it's all your fault, you asked for it.* Over time, if you live with your adrenaline system on constant alert because you never know what's going to set the china flying—if you live with that much stress, forever vigilant for that cloud the size of a man's hand that's going to turn into a storm you have to fend off, for the kids' sake—over time, your brain's biochemical pathways get rearranged. The circuitry gets rewired, as it does after you've borne your first child. And the changes are apt to be permanent.

I'm lucky; I have a mildish case of PTSD, rarely disabling, and most of the time it's pretty low-key. The startle reflex is its best index; the higher I jump at a loud noise, the more into PTSD I am. Sometimes I hardly jump at all. This is likely going to be the way things are from now until I cross the River into the next life. I hope and believe in healing. I cannot expect to be fixed.

But it's a great gift, in a cross-eyed sort of way. I cannot help knowing that I'm wounded; it's too obvious, especially on the bad days. There's nothing like being thoroughly broken to knock the stuffing out of your egotism, but that's precisely what we all need, because egotism stands between the self and God like an eclipsing moon. The granddaddy of the Seven Deadly Sins is Pride (meaning not rightful pride, but the need to feel good about yourself regardless of what it costs). That sort of Pride is not something you have a lot of in this situation. I now have a label pasted to me, *psychiatric disorder*, and this label (unlike some others) is a true and accurate descriptor and therefore almost more a comfort than an upset.

If you know you're broken, you can accept the help you need to be healed. If you know that you yourself can never fully be put back to rights, because the past is past and can't be undone, you can accept the brokenness of others more gracefully and lovingly.

Members of this club of broken people know what matters and what does not. This is why Christ told the broken, in the Beatitudes, how lucky they are: "Blessed are those who mourn." It isn't a feel-good cheer-up statement, a Pollyannaish bit of upbeat fiction; it's a statement of fact. We *are* blessed, we who are wounded and know it. We didn't choose to be here, but the spiritual landscape is surprisingly rich and interesting.

It's a choice, what you can do with this stuff—it's always a choice. Some things, like sex or nuclear power or long suffering, carry great power: the question is what you're going to do with that power—use it for God's ends or for your own sneaky self-satisfying purposes, for control or destruction or revenge or puffing up your own ego at someone else's expense. I could be Lot's wife, forever staring back over my shoulder, turned into a bitter, pure-white pillar. But salt's dead. I don't want to be that way. I did plenty of dead in the past, and I don't intend to go back there ever again.

God tugs me Godward, and Godward is also lifeward, and that entails a fair bit of suffering as well as joy. For suffering and joy are really only two sides of the same coin—the coin of love, pure gold, not the brilliant fool's stuff with its peacocky sheen. I'll have it this way, thank you.

I sit in my screen house, the sides flapping gently in this small-town quiet, and all these elements lie about me on the grass—they and others, some I can only dimly discern. I know there are elements that I can't even begin to imagine. I also know that there are elements that don't fit into the pattern I am starting to discern: I am, after all, a wife, a sister, a daughter, a mother, holder-down of a number of jobs, owner of a house and co-vivant with four cats. I can't keep all of these strands busy in the pattern, any more than I can listen to all the musical lines in Bach's great Kyrie in the *Mass in B Minor*: as soon as I pick up one voice and start to follow it through, I lose another voice.

We know God only "through a glass, darkly"—well, the same goes for our own lives, given the sloppiness of memory, the wild imprecision of the human heart. Only later will I see God as God sees me, and see myself as God sees me too. For right now, all I have to play with is a group of elements sitting here on the brown grass inside four cheap plastic walls: my dependence on God, my need for the Spirit to guide and direct me, my knowledge of my own ignorance, my acceptance of woundedness as natural and even necessary. All I can do is to bring forth the small figures that grace and compose my own cross.

It's a start. Will that do, Lord?

# THE BUG

There is a green bug on the screen of my laptop. I know it's alive, because it changes position every now and again as the breeze sweeps through the screen house, but it is being quite remarkably quiet. Presumably something about the screen attracts it; Lord only knows what subtle electromagnetic fields an elderly IBM ThinkPad's screen gives off. But the green bug is as peaceful as a sleeping cat. I have no idea what kind of green bug it is; I'll have to ask my friendly neighborhood naturalists.

What's remarkable about the green bug is its color: a brilliant iridescent enamel green—presumably it spends most of its time in grass or leaves and this color is adaptive. On my screen, on the other hand, it is splendidly startling: a Fabergé jewel pinned to a business suit's gray lapel. I keep having to stop work to lean closer and examine it: surfaces, the miniature legs, the neatly folded transparent wings, the glitter of light bouncing off the curves of its tiny thorax. Of course, any living being is a walking (waddling, swimming, flying, sessile) miracle, and that goes for earwigs as well as iridescent green bugs. But a being that's beautiful in our eyes—and this really is a *very* beautiful green bug, I can tell you—seems doubly miraculous. You can watch it and reflect how long it took people to be able to create anything this beautiful, this perfect—and our creations lack the ultimate perfection. They aren't alive.

Meanwhile, a dragonfly sails slowly around the screen house—which isn't, of course, particularly bugproof (we expected?). No fools, dragonflies. This one has scented people, and people mean mosquitoes and mosquitoes mean lunch. I have seen dragonflies gather like a flotilla around a hiker setting off into the woods in blackfly season, thirty or forty of them fanning out, vanguard, flanking forces, rear guard. Whenever I see dragonflies I remember how ancient they are, and how practical: they feel like a blessing whenever I see them.

Nature never makes me feel insignificant: if the green bug matters, then so do I. If the dragonfly has its purposeful life, then so can I. Either God goes for size and brilliance and only values great important things at the galactic level—which I strongly doubt—or God has a deep abiding affection for all his creation, this brilliant green bug and the dragonfly and me. I'm grateful to have studied biology, not cosmology: you get an idea of how purely *neat*

Creation is, if you study it at the micro level. I can regard this green bug and know that its thread-thick legs are capable of intense biochemical activity, that its body is frantically metabolizing, that its small transparent wings can manage stunning feats of flight. This green bug is a miracle. And so am I.

Nature doesn't make me feel puny and unworthy, but it does have a way of putting things into perspective. If I have troubles and worries, I can bring them out here and compare them to the spruce trees. Spruces aren't (by tree standards) any great shakes for longevity; an old spruce might be seventy years. But these trees were there long before any of my troubles started, and they will be here long after the current crop has become not just history but completely irrelevant.

There's a steadiness in the aged ground beneath my feet, something I can rest on, secure. The limestone under this soil goes back half a billion years or so. And not so far from here is the Canadian Shield, the oldest rock in the world and some of the toughest. This bug may die in a week or two; I will certainly die in such and such number of years; the world will fall into the sun eventually, and even this rock will melt. Does it all have Existential Meaning or Not? That's our own fretful choice. The bug is simply being a bug.

The green bug is rubbing its forelegs together—why, I don't know. It looks almost like a washing or grooming motion, but it might be that the bug is tasting its environment, sensing what interesting molecules are borne about on the air. I don't understand the bug, and it doesn't understand me; and that too is oddly comforting—I'm not defending dug-in ignorance here, just accepting that there are things I don't know about. I don't have to under-stand everything, not even flies. I can't understand anything, really; it's all mystery, what goes on at the center of things. Maybe to a scientist this is irritating or unnerving. To me, it's being let off the hook: if I choose to believe in God, as I have done again and again, then I can trust that God knows not only what I haven't learned about yet but what I can never possibly understand. For which I thank God.

My house's three big maples have a root in three centuries now; in their time, generations have been born, grown, wed, bred, and died. Looked at in one way, this proves the futility and fruitless-ness of life: we are but grass, here a little while and then gone without a trace, grumblegrumblegrumblesnort. It's an easy attitude to take if you believe, in your secret inmost depth, that you're *re-ally* the only significant entity in the universe and that when you go, the whole shebang loses any vestige of meaning, because the light of the world has been switched off.

Is this life all (as those great romantics, the cynics, would have it) a great waste of time and energy, for no discernible purpose? "A tale told by an idiot, full of sound and fury / Signifying noth-ing." I can't say one way or another: maybe they have it right and I am a naive, self-deceiving idiot for having faith at all, much less faith that this beauty does matter, does have some meaning, even if I don't necessarily know what it is. But it seems a pity to waste the sight of a really beautiful green bug sitting quietly on my lap-top screen on the most perfect of June afternoons, the gentle air full of these ordinary sounds, just to be intellectually respectable. (Is it harder to be cynical if you're an exurbanite? I wonder.)

It's one of the many side benefits of believing in God, knowing that the green bug will die and die shortly, green-bug life spans being as they are; but for the moment, it's just sitting on my screen being utterly beautiful. And this moment exists in eternity. For now, I can try to wrap this moment and this fly up in memory, as in amber, to be stowed away with my earrings and coral necklace, but I'm transient too. Everything is, except for God. It's only a matter of degree: the green bug, Max-cat rolling in the grass, me, my maple trees, the limestone, this world. We all began in time and will end in time, sooner or later. But we all matter, for we are all God's creation and we are greatly loved, simply for that reason, and that love will roll on throughout time and right out the other side of it.

I trust happily that when I die, this ground beneath my feet will go on, and other feet will tread it. Max will die, and other cats (even other gray tabby neutered toms, perhaps) will patrol this turf, beating up intruders and terrorizing the field mice. This green bug will definitely die; I could slay it with a fingertip (fat chance!). But bottle-green bugs will inhabit this landscape on other June afternoons. And my maples' scions are sprouting in the field next door.

I'd rather glory in whatever's right under my nose, glorying also in the fact that it will be here when I'm gone—it or its successors. It's a relief to consider myself only a temporary part of this landscape—significant, because even the grass matters, because the dragonfly matters, the green bug matters. That's quite enough. Anything more would be frosting on the cake.

Yet I know in my bones that there is and will be more: that because I have the capacity to choose, to feel, and to love or its opposite, as the green bug can't, I do have a level of significance that the green bug doesn't have. I have been given talents and abilities that my maples lack, and I have the duty to make of them something that does honor to their Creator—to return them to their giver, with a little extra added on for gratitude's sake. I do know that.

But just for now, I think I'd rather sit with the green bug and the dragonfly, with Max-cat (who has stretched out on the grass in what looks like a state of total bliss), with the pair of crows squawking through the spruces and the screen house flapping gently in the breeze. "To everything there is a season and a time for every purpose under heaven," and this is clearly a time to admire iridescent bottle-green bugs. And that's what I should be doing.

*I did call my friendly neighborhood naturalists later, and they told me that my green bug is a halictine bee, probably the genus* Augochlora, *a harmless critter that lives in hard-packed soil or old wood. Like other bees, it will sting but only if provoked. As best they can tell, it was stoned out of its gourd on my laptop screen's electromagnetic radiation.*

PSALM 131

*O Lord, my heart is not lifted up,*
*my eyes are not raised too high;*
*I do not occupy myself with things*
*too great and too marvelous for me.*
*But I have calmed and quieted my soul,*
*like a weaned child with its mother;*
*my soul is like the weaned child that is with me.*
*O Israel, hope in the Lord*
*from this time on and forevermore.*

I am in church now. I rise and stand or sit or kneel with the others, at the appointed places in the liturgy, so familiar now that my movements are mostly unconscious. When it comes time to sing, I place my voice carefully, using a fraction of its full power, trying to capture the notes accurately and to sing smoothly and correctly, and again, this is mostly unconscious. If you sing in choir, there's a discipline and technique that you internalize: listening for the accompaniment and the other parts, keeping an eye on the director.

The fact that my voice and body are now so disciplined, so at ease with this liturgy, leaves my soul free to do what it's here for. I go into a quiet place where time slows to a deeply satisfying crawl. I am sitting now, ears, attention, and mind intently listening to the sermon (our rector is an excellent preacher), but another part of me has gone off to crawl into God's arms—that weaned child on mama's lap again. The service that when I was a child seemed interminable now feels like a warm refuge that I'm in no particular hurry to leave. I like the fact that it takes its own good time. I feel held here, suspended comfortably, and I know that God is busy about my soul as I dangle in time—that I am being nourished and cared for in this time, so that when it draws naturally to its conclusion, I will be able to go forth into the world all furbished up and fed.

This is *opus dei,* the work of God—not God's work in me, but the work I owe to God. Only it doesn't feel in the least like work, not now. If it was work before, acquiring the discipline, that's long over and done with. It's the easiest thing in the world now, just being in this stillness, this deep peace. It costs nothing—only the willingness to be attentive, the desire to be here. It's taken quite a while, but I've finally understood that truly, all God ever asked of me was to turn in my paces and look in his direction.

I know, however, that I can't seem to make this state-of-being happen. There's another part of me that can be fidgety as a hyper small child, slipping off in all directions, incapable of paying proper attention. And when I'm like that, I can't enter this peace where I find nourishment. I'm not capable of focusing on God; I'm too distractible. I have to accept that this is part of my humanity; while I can try to control the twitchiness, I can't entirely make it go away. But I know that God knows that it isn't the way I want to be. I want to be peaceful, a tired child on my Father's lap.

I am in a small white-painted office in the city, and I am talking with Mary, my spiritual director. She is gently teasing God-images out of me, one after another, and we are both laughing with delight. The images are brilliantly vivid and alive. I imagine stowing them all away in a piratical treasure chest like a child's collection of marbles, heaps and piles of God-images, ready to spill and roll out, fetching up in corners and under the sofa. I imagine God picking one of my image-marbles up and rolling it around in the palm of his hand, admiring my admiration.

The images are awash in color—rich blues and emeralds, crimsons and deep peach, the true deep gold of dandelions, shot through with light. I know there are colors there that my eyes cannot see—unimaginable color. I know there will be rich music there, scents and perfumes, the rustle of leaves, thunderstorms—everything that is vivid and alive, imaginative, outrageous, sharply alive.

For God is anything but sterile, and "the foolishness of God is greater than the wisdom of man." I want God to be foolish. I want being-in-God to involve a certain amount of Dionysian giggling, rude snorts, pennywhistles piping through woods where there are bonfires blazing and figures leaping in very ancient dances. Maybe others want God to be black-and-white, a figure of neat divisions and clear-cut Law, but I want God to be in flagrant swirling Technicolor. I have seen what it is to be A Very Good Girl, and I'm not sure that's what God's goodness is like. I think maybe God's goodness has a fair streak of mischief. Or so I hope.

*A*mong my God-images there is one very different from the others; a friend gave it to me when I was first on my own, raw and desperate—a self-employed single mother trying to haul the whole household along single-handed, while all the abuse issues were surfacing and I was still dealing with the kids' reactions to their parents' breakup. It was bad, very bad. I used to drive to places where I couldn't possibly be overheard and sit in my car, pounding on the steering wheel and yelling a lot, because you can have a complete nervous breakdown in your car, as long as the ignition's off. It's a safe place.

My friend Jake, who had been there, done that, offered me her image of God: of the Lamb with thick, springy fleece that you could drive your face into, twisting your fingers hard into the curling wool, letting its roughness scrub the tears off your cheeks and the snot from your nose—the Lamb has no objection to grappling, desperate fingers and snotty noses. Still, sometimes, even though life is so much better, I like to go back to that image, curling my fingers deep in the rough lanolined wool, leaning my cheek up against its warmth.

know how it feels having a tired tod-
dler on your lap. They're so busy, so intent, playing intensely, roar-
ing or beaming, but going full blast—and then the tiredness
catches up, and they want to sit on your lap being read to quietly.
That weight, so completely relaxed, the small starfish hand lying
on your wrist as your voice finds the cadence of the poem or slips
into the familiar rhythm of a story you've already read a gazillion
times . . . and then the head is heavy against your shoulder and upper arm, and you lay down the book and hoist the soft, warm,
bonelessness off for a nap—or just sit there, holding the sleeping
child. I used to do that, just sit and hold. Even then, I knew I
wouldn't have this forever. Grab it before it's gone.

But to be as a weaned child—I don't know if I can do that. I'm
an adult, but I'm also a grown-up; the two aren't quite the same.
For a moment or two in church, I can still my own busy inquir-
ing mind and be at peace, but can I really lean back, as my drowsy
small sons used to lean back in my arms, trusting that God's
shoulder will be there behind my head and God's arm will be
folded close around me? I wish I could.

# THE OXBOW

At this distance, I can't be completely sure which summer it was: the summer I turned nine or the summer I turned ten. Both years, we spent a couple of weeks at the house of a friend-family in an obscure rural township in the uppermost Berkshires, just under the Vermont border.

The Oxbow—it's actually got a proper road name, but everyone calls it the Oxbow—lay at the top of the township, uphill from everything and everyone else, and in this particular township, uphill is upHILL. The road passed the town cemetery and dived into the woods, through groves of white birch rising up from beds of fern, past immense and dignified pines. The roadbed was, in some places, dug down below the forest floor by the annual passage of the road scraper. It twisted casually past lichened boulders, dropped ages ago by the glaciers. Driving along it, you had to slow down as the road itself dived over patches of surfacing rock.

In the eighteenth century, the land on either side of the Oxbow had been painfully cleared and farmed. You could still see the foundations of houses long since fallen in, and the long stone walls snaking off into the re-sprung forest. But little of the land in the township is much good for farming, and a century before, people had given up and moved west, where the land was decently horizontal, if less decorative, and had more than two inches of soil over rock. Now there were only the two old houses where there had once been more. Just past the eighteenth-century farmhouse where my family were guests, the road itself gave up the struggle and dwindled down to a mere path, turning east and looping around through the woods before widening out again to become a road on the other side.

I think it was early afternoon. I was alone. I don't know where my sisters were—gone into town with a parent, perhaps. The other grown-ups were all indoors. I let myself out the back door, walked barefoot across the lawn (my mother never insisted on shoes unless it was necessary), and turned down to where the road Oxbow ended and the path Oxbow started. I walked down the path a bit, far enough that the house was well behind me. And there I stopped and stood, staring into the woods, breathing in their particular smell of damp and ferns.

My family had just come through Interesting Times: the precarious harmony between my parents, based on sheer determination, abstract goodness, and a painfully one-sided sort of love, had shattered when my father behaved badly and almost lost his job. My mother had had to intervene on his behalf in ways that hurt and humiliated her. Their marriage, never a good one, had come very close to falling apart. I didn't know that at the time. All my sisters and I knew was that something had gone very wrong in unspoken ways that left us confused and uncertain and hurting. At the same time, we'd left Illinois and moved East, into a suburban society where we felt judged, friendless, and lost. We'd all suffered, and we'd done our suffering separately, silently, partly because you didn't talk about these things then; but also because my father didn't want the matter spoken of, and he always had a way of getting whatever he wanted.

I was still carrying all that with me as I walked slowly down the path and stopped and stared deep into the woods. I had never seen such woods before. I don't think I'd seen much of woods anywhere: only the flatness of Illinois, suburban Connecticut, and the rocks of the Maine coast, where we'd spent vacations with my cousins. I'd never been turned loose in a landscape like this, so still, so deeply green, so full of peace.

*I*t was almost forty years later that I learned more about the township where the Oxbow was: how, some twenty years before I first saw it, it had attracted a colony of brilliant and holy people. Reinhold Niebuhr had summered there, and he'd first spoken the Serenity Prayer in the bare white clapboard church on the plain unpicturesque village green. Eminent and thoughtful clergy—theologians, teachers, and bishops of the liberal wing of the American Episcopalian and Presbyterian churches—had formed a sort of colony, buying up the old houses, bringing their kids up for the summer and entertaining their distinguished guests—people like W. H. Auden and Isaiah Berlin and Felix Frankfurter.

I don't know if there was something about the place that attracted people of faith, or whether the faith of these people had somehow leaked into the landscape, making it holy—the way you can sometimes feel prayer leaking out of the walls of good churches. But there was a Something there, in those hills and mountains. Celtic Christianity talks of Thin Places, places where God and the earth get unusually close, and Aboriginal peoples have their holy places, places which they find spiritually rich and significant. This place felt like one of those.

I didn't know any of that as I stood curling my bare brown toes into the soft, deep moss and staring off into the woods. I only knew that somehow the land itself, or the woods, or whatever spirit inhabited this place, was sucking the misery out of me like venom from a wound. I felt the hurt and confusion drain from me, flowing down into the moss and among the tree roots, the way you can sometimes feel fatigue draining away from your body into your mattress when you lie down exhausted. The sense of loneliness that had ached so badly turned quietly and sweetly into a contented pleasure in my own company and the company of whatever it was that was lurking in the landscape.

Above all I had a strong sense that Joy was out there somewhere: at the other end of the Oxbow path, perhaps, or maybe
over the next ridge, or a mile deeper into the woods. Where exactly didn't matter. I had no urgent need to find Joy, and with a
child's wisdom I knew better than to go looking. Any perceptive
child learns early that anticipation is a whole lot more fun than
possession. I knew it was there, and I knew it knew I was there,
and we were companionable in this fresh awareness.

At the same time, I knew, quite suddenly, that I had a being of
my own: I was not only my parents' daughter, the middle one of
three, a granddaughter and niece and cousin and grade school student, a child with curly hair who already wrote poetry. I was
Molly. There was—I knew it from the woods—a Mollyness of
Molly that tasted totally unlike any other flavor of person, that
was distinct and particular and completely one of a kind. I knew
myself to be separate and apart from every other person in the
world, even my sisters.

This new apartness didn't feel lonely; it felt deliciously secret.
No other soul's toes could feel the deep moss in quite this particular way. No other soul could look into these woods and see what
I was seeing. No other soul could smell the ferny dampness as I
could at that moment. There was Joy on the other side of the hill,
and a small girl with curly brown hair standing in a clearing, and
the two of us were alone with each other and utterly happy.

I knew that I wanted that Joy, and that Joy wanted me. But at
the same time, both of us were strangely content to have a slight
distance between us, for the time being, like two old and happy

lovers sitting across the table from each other, peacefully not troubling to hold hands or touch each other, because they know that later they'll be between the sheets, skin to skin.

*T*hat was a couple of lifetimes ago, or so it feels. Now, as I stand in my kitchen, I find myself suddenly hijacked, bowled over, sprung upon by a brilliant light happiness, the equivalent, moodwise, of the yellow at the very center of a fullblown dandelion. These moments catch me, and I feel held in them momentarily, endlessly. They pass, and the normal strains and problems are still there. But just for a moment, now and again, I feel as though I have been mugged by Joy.

This feeling comes back: I got jumped by it a few weeks back, if you can get jumped by something as thick and deep amber as honey. I thought: *It's so good to have you back; will you stay with me a little while?* But Joy needs to get around, to be spread. We shouldn't be jealous or possessive. Let this moment happen, it said; don't ask it to wait until you've got time for it, but don't try to hold on to it either. It may need to get on along to the next person who's waiting.

*F*orty years after that moment on the Oxbow, and I have come back to the same area in the mountains, to a campground in the next township. Now I am sitting at a picnic table in a sandy pine wood, surrounded by deciduous undergrowth through which the light shines like jewelry. Around me are the usual things: propane stove and lamp, green hex tent, blue plastic tarps forming surprisingly effective shelters. The mountains here grow so close that you think if you leaned sideways, you could lay your cheek against their flanks. The river sounds at my back, in full spate with all this rain. While the showers are spectacular here—when it rains, it *rains*—I have to say that by Canadian standards the local mosquitoes are wusses, pale imitations of the Real Thing. They seem to circle your wrist, shyly requesting permission to land. Huh.

Two days ago I went back up to the Oxbow; we climbed up into the mountains and drove down past the town cemetery, down the old road to the farmhouse where I stayed as a child. The same family still owns it, the family we stayed with all those years ago. I always thought that when I die I'd like to have my ashes brought out to that green mossy path, with the ferns and the old stone wall snaking through the woods. It never occurred to me that this too might be changeable.

Offhand, I'd say it looks like lumbering. The woods in this township are mostly managed timberlot; every so many years, contractors' crew open up rough tracks into the woods, so they can take the heavy equipment in and take out the mature trees. We used to lumber our own land, when we owned the white house here. If it's done properly, it does the woods no harm at all; but for a while, until the ferns and moss creep back and the younger trees fill out, the landscape looks a little raw in places.

They must have lumbered here quite recently: the heavy-equipment track marks are printed neat and deep in the mud at the margins of what used to be the path. What had been a road and become a path is a road once again, slashing a newly brown course into woods that now lack the tall canopy that gave them such depth and richness—you need the big trees for that.

This time, back in my growing-up places, I visited both my houses: the brick house next to the church, where we lived during the school year, and the white frame house downhill from here, where we spent the summers. Both have been extensively and unhappily mucked about with; I don't think I'd recognize them anymore, except for the outsides. And now the Oxbow.

I could indulge in a tasty little peroration of despair: "Change and decay are all about us." I could have a nice wallow in the Transience of Things, perhaps with a side order of Meaninglessness and Existential Anguish. More legitimately, I could be doing some real mourning: these places were precious to me, and now they've been altered out of all recognition. And yes, for a moment, my eyes did sting and water as I looked for that light and realized that it was gone.

But you can't go back to Eden; you can only go on to Zion. Maybe the lesson I'm supposed to take to heart here is that I'm not meant to hang on to the fugitive past. But perhaps the flip side of that lesson is that in the long run the past is not meant to hang on to me, or at least not forever. That's something to hope for.

It may be that in twenty or thirty years' time, some other child will stand here curling bare toes into the moss, and by then the young trees will have grown and filled in and the road will be at least more weathered, less abruptly new. Maybe, maybe not. Whoever that child is, it won't be me. I doubt very much that by the time the beauty returns to this place I'll be around to stare into it again. *My* Oxbow is gone, for now.

But I have it still in the whole shape of my soul; it's stamped into me, one of the earliest seals of all the ones I carry on my dog-eared personal pages. Sorrows will come and go, but all joys are, I believe, permanent; they are recorded in God's time and will be there when we find ourselves on the other side of the River—only then they will be far stronger, truer, more deeply colored, than anything we could have experienced in this life. So in that sense, I really don't have anything to mourn for. And I don't, in fact, feel sad.

The stumps in the piney woods we're camping in—they show where trees were here before and were cut down long ago. The tall straight pines that replaced them will themselves be replaced by trees as yet unsprouted. From shrew to mountain, we're all on the move in time, at whatever rate, and our time goes strictly forward toward mortality: the field mouse curled up in a tussock of grass, the earth falling into the sun. But God's time is different from ours. And God alone knows how any one moment, of whatever significance, can spread its implications around the landscape.

The joy is the important thing, and I find it here around me in the campsite, in the light flickering through the brilliant leaves and the tall dark pine boles and the sound of water. I find it in my screen house too. It isn't just in that one particular place and time; it is before, behind, around, above, and below me. I may not always be aware of it, but it is always aware of me, and it knows it will get me in the end. Only a matter of time.

*Part Two*

# STILL LIFE, WITH DRAGONS

*Portraits, Somewhat Fictional*

# WOMAN AT THE WELL

The other women would have come early in the cool of the day, chattering companionably as they let down their water jars into the well. Here she is at noon, alone except for the quiet dusty man sitting on the stonework. She is doing this hard, heavy work in the heat of the day, when everybody else is indoors having a siesta. She is here at noon because if she came early, with the other women, she'd have to endure their looks and comments. She has enough to do coping with the steady running commentary from the monkey of self-blame who sits on her shoulder, the beast invisible to all but her, who natters incessantly at her, chewing away at her. She doesn't need any outside commentary. So she stays away from the other women, because there's nothing like *that* look in a respectable woman's eyes to make another woman feel like a piece of garbage.

Her history isn't recorded in any great detail, so we don't know what had happened to her. Maybe she'd simply had a run of terrible luck, like Job before her. Perhaps she'd been repeat-edly widowed or repudiated, through no fault of her own—infer-tility, perhaps, or family alliances coming unglued. That's what some respectable scholars say might have happened. But the women I know say: *Huh. This one's been around the block a few too many times.*

She will see in others' eyes, then, condemnation, or superiority, or the sweet falseness of conventional sympathy, or perhaps fear—people can't help believing that bad luck is catching; there must be an evil eye somewhere, and what if it chances to glance in your direction? People also don't know what to do with someone who's damaged, whether by bad choices or sheer chance. They feel awk-ward and uncomfortable. They are attracted to the happy and suc-cessful, and the happy and successful are not out here drawing water at midday, in this dusty place with the dusty quiet man. So she lives alone in town, with the man with whom she has no rights except the right to be looked down on and held at fault for what-ever. And that just makes her lonelier.

The funny thing is, it really doesn't matter whether or not she's been promiscuous or just unlucky. Even if she's perfectly innocent, she's had Job's comforters, within and without, saying, "Since God is just, if you keep running into all these problems, surely there must be something you've done to deserve them." And if she casts her mind back and sees that she hasn't done anything to deserve what happened, or not nearly enough, then Job's comforters inside and outside will whisper to her, "Well, if it isn't something you've done, it must be *who you are*. There's something made all wrong in you, something you can't see yourself that attracts trouble as rotting meat attracts flies. There must be."

And that's where the terrible damage gets done, and it's all the worse because what's damaged and dirty is her sexuality, her womanness, where she is most vulnerable and can be made to feel hopelessly unclean. Whether or not she's done wrong, the sense of wrongness sinks in over time; it seems to seep into her being like spilled lamp oil into wood; it gets so mixed up in the fibers of herself that there's no way on God's earth she could ever be cleaned or made whole. She dreams that God, finding no way to separate out her wrongness from her self, will have to burn the two together—that to undo whatever the wrongness is, she herself will have to be sacrificed. At least that's what she dreams, in nightmares that set her bolt upright beside the heavy man with whom she has no rights, gasping and praying frantically to a God who is absolutely silent.

Sometimes, in her own house, when she's alone, she can think back to when she was young, before it all went wrong. She can remember having been worth something, having had some value; she can recollect when the world was a promising place and what awaited her was a man of her own, a house, children, a place in her world, the honor a good woman can have even in a world that doesn't honor women. And then it's not so bad. But sometimes all she can do then is to mourn what she lost—or, rather, mourn what she was never given to lose. You can't mourn the loss of love if you've never been properly loved; you can only mourn the fact that you have never had it to mourn for. But who understands that, except those who have been in the same position?

Walking across to the well is when the shame hits her hardest, because she feels most exposed and loneliest then. Her water jar may be heavy, but her sense of shame is heavier still; it always is. Shame is such dense stuff, much, much heavier than mere guilt. Even quite small balls of shame weigh you down, so that you struggle to walk across the village square or climb a set of stairs. It pushes your head down, bowing your shoulders forward, or it makes you walk unnaturally upright, your shoulder blades so rigidly yanked back that they ache, a clench in your upper back, and your molars crunched together. It's that heavy, shame.

So she walks across the dusty square, grim and silent, and there's this dusty, quiet man sitting on the masonry around the well. There are only the two of them there, although God alone knows how many are watching them from the silent midday houses. It is intensely quiet, only the buzz of insects and the lonely caw of a distant crow. She steps quietly, not wishing to draw attention to herself. After a quick, sideways glance, she keeps her eyes off him. She can see from his clothing that he's a Jew, not a Samaritan, and she's down enough already, she doesn't need his ritual contempt. She fancies he can tell what she is anyway; a respectable woman wouldn't be out here at this time of day, on her own. She's had enough put-downs. She'll just get her water and go before he can lecture her or spit at her or just give her one of those looks.

But astonishingly, she hears his voice; he is speaking to her, not *at* her, *to* her, quite matter-of-factly, without any unkindness or condescension in his tone. He is asking her for a drink of water. This is so startling that she looks at him involuntarily, and she sees no contempt in his face either. He is just a person with a thirst, and she is just a person with a water jar, which she almost dropped just now, and he is asking her for a drink from the well. Him drink from *her* jar? Is he really such a fool as that? Doesn't he realize that the very clay is unclean to him? Again, involuntarily, she blurts out, "How is it that a Jew can ask for a drink from a woman of Samaria?"

And then something even more surprising: he shifts subject abruptly, engaging her, really *talking* to her, as though she were a person of worth, making her an offer of something precious: "If you knew who I am, *you'd* ask *me* for a drink, and the water I would give you is living water." She's bewildered: "How could you give me a drink? You don't have a jar to let down into the well. Are you greater than Jacob, whose well this was?" "If you drink the water I have to give you, you will never be thirsty again." By now she's completely at sea. But the notion of not having to fetch water again, not having to take that long solitary shame-laden hike from her house to the well—oh, what she'd give to be let off that particular chore. She grabs at the idea, and at the kindliness of his voice, clutching eagerly at a small straw of hope. "Oh, give me that water, so that I may never have to be thirsty or come back to this well again."

"Bring your husband here," he says, out of nowhere, and for a second she's stunned, and then the pain kicks in. She should have known better. She should have known that even if he seemed to accept her as a woman and a Samaritan, and treated her without contempt for those parts of herself that he had every right to despise—even if he could accept all that, he'd still see the wrongness in her, that stain soaked in, too deep to be removed. That's why he asks about her husband. He knows. He can see what everyone else can see, the wrong-something-in-her that's so sunk into her being that nothing can ever separate it out and get rid of it. Oh, well; that's just the way it goes, has always gone, will always go. Her lie ("I have no husband") is mechanical, a puff of air as hope collapses once again around her ears—you'd think a person would get used to this, eventually. . . .

But his voice, listing her past that he could not possibly know about, stays as kind and level as it had been. He is still *talking* to her, not naming and blaming the wrongness, but simply telling her that yes, he already does know about all that stuff, and really it isn't important. Or it's important because it's caused her so much suffering, and he knows about the suffering too, and the guilt and the weight of shame. He knows of that healthy hopeful girl who used to be, and he knows that that girl is really who she still is— but he also knows how she got to be where she is now, what choices, what chances fetched her to this dusty place under a merciless sun. But none of this is part of *her;* she has a self worthy of love. This wrongfulness is like dirt on a mirror: on, not in, the glass. Something that can be cleaned away.

*He knows. He has really seen her, exactly as she is. And he's still talking to her.*

Can't you see, you people who see only a dusty man and a woman with a water jar talking together—can't you see that what he is doing is pulling that stain out of her, so that they can both set it down and walk away from it? He is sorting through her self and cleaning the crud out: the old mistakes, the old tragedies, the corrosive self-blame, all the times she's been found at fault and accepted the fault when in fact she shouldn't have. He's picking all of that out of her, and he's telling her that when the wrong's all picked out, there is still a person there, a real person, as valuable and beloved as the highest priest in Jerusalem—a woman of Samaria, who should have had it so much easier.

He is looking her in the eyes now and telling her that she *exists,* outside the wrongfulness she thought was part of herself, as much her as the shape of her hand. And if he's right, if the wrongfulness isn't really *her,* then maybe it doesn't have to rule the rest of her life. Maybe things can be different.

And yes, there is living water. She knows now what it tastes like.

# THE MAN WITH THE TRAY
# OF TILES

Looking back, of course I was terminally naive. I knew nothing of cyberspace or Netiquette; the term "flame war" had never crossed my personal screen, and I hadn't a clue what "FWIW" or "ROTFLMHO" meant, much less "IMNSHO." I wouldn't have known a sig file or a listserv if one had up and bit me. I'd only gotten the modem for my computer at my boss's urging, so that I could toss files back and forth with the office quickly and easily via the Internet. My boss (he who has been into computers since he built his first one from a Heathkit back in the late Mesozoic and who would rather surf the Net than breathe) knew about my weird preoccupation with this religion stuff and thought I might be interested in Christian discussion groups, so he dug up some information and passed it along to me. I found a group that looked interesting and respectable—an Anglican forum on Christian Ethics—and got myself signed on.

I found myself tossed instantly into a high-powered discussion of the Question of Homosexuality: is it a natural sexual orientation, or is it a sinful perverted "lifestyle choice"? Again, naiveté: I don't think it had ever crossed my mind to see homosexuality as inherently sinful. I have homosexual friends and relatives, and it wouldn't occur to me to reject them for that, any more than I could reject them for being left-handed or blue-eyed. Yes, some homosexual people could behave badly, I knew that—but so can heterosexual people. Sexual sin exists; it involves using other people's bodies for one's own sexual satisfaction without caritas or concern for the other. I'd known gay couples who'd been together for years, and they looked like heterosexual couples who'd been together for years. I'd also known gay friends who'd been around the block too many times; ditto straights. I could see how much harder life was for them than for me, and how that might affect them in ways that they got wrongly judged for. But I couldn't for a moment see them as other than people.

After reading the other members' contributions (called "posts," on electronic mailing lists) for a while, I could start seeing what the opposite arguments were, and how some people might have legitimate questions in need of answers and concerns that needed to be addressed ("If we don't draw the line at heterosexual marriage, where do we draw the line?"). I've run into all sorts of conservative clergypersons discussing sexual ethics, and I understand their position tolerably well. What this group needed was a civilized, reasonable, thoughtful discussion rooted in sound information, respect for the opponent, and charity, which is what you might expect from an Anglican forum on Christian Ethics. But that's not what I got. In fact, what I got scared me considerably.

The discussion, if that's what you want to call it, was being conducted by a small group of gay men on one side and two (male) Anglican priests on the other. The gay men struck me as being remarkably patient, forbearing, restrained, and courteous given the provocation they were being given. The priests' posts, on the other hand, were like something you'd turn up under a rotten log. They were full of a vicious, visceral hatefulness, coupled with scatological side comments verging on pornography that shocked the bejayzus out of me. They were purely venomous. I have never, before or since, had such a sudden wild impulse to scrub out my computer modem with yellow soap and to fumigate it with burning sulfur.

I am a preacher's kid, and I know as well as any and better than most that clergy are first and foremost human beings, quite capable of belching, scratching, playing power politics, drinking too much, and making extremely dumb mistakes. The male variety puts his pants on one leg at a time and the female model probably has problems with her bra straps, just like the rest of us. I don't expect clergy to be saintly. Hell, I don't expect saints to be saintly. Saints know better than the rest of us just how human they are, just as saints know better than the rest of us how we all stray from the beliefs we profess.

But these priests' posts were well past ordinary clergy-type boo-

boos; they were right over the line into Really, Truly Evil, fairly concentrated. Read them, and you couldn't help thinking of some of the nastier and more scatological anti-Semitic literature produced by the Third Reich. I don't expect priests to be perfect, but there are limits, and these guys had crossed them and were well into the next county. I got a friend, Max, to look at the posts, just in case I was overreacting, and he had the same impression: these were scary.

The posts pushed Max and me right through disgusted, scared, and angry and out the other side into sheer puzzlement. We looked at each other and asked simultaneously, "How? Why?" How could two men dedicated to the service of God, reading the Gospel every week, write this sewage?

There's a word, praxis, for describing the sort of behavior in which your walk and your talk are closely aligned. You take the theory in your right hand and your own behavior in your left hand and you look from one to the other, seeing how well the one conforms to the other. If there's a major difference and you have any sort of reasonable sense of honor, either you have to dump your theory and stick with your actions or you have to remodel your behavior to conform better to your theory.

But sometimes, as in the case of these two grossly homophobic priests, the person fails to make any sort of real connection between theory and practice. Some people call this hypocrisy. And hypocrisy does exist: it exists when a person thinks, "Yes, there are those beliefs I hold, but they don't really apply in the real world" or "It's nice to be so idealistic, but we have to be practical." It's the notion that somehow Sunday is special and separate and apart from what we do on Monday—that walk and talk don't have to be related. We do see a gap between the two; we just don't think it's a problem worth dealing with.

I'm not sure, in this case, that that's what was going on. Hypocrisy is like lying; it includes some sort of intentional deceit or dishonesty. But if you say something wrong genuinely believing it to be true, you aren't lying; you're making a mistaken statement. If you don't see any real discrepancy between your walk and your talk when there is, in fact, quite a noticeable gap between the two, I don't think you're being a hypocrite; I think you've got a serious blind spot. So, on the grounds that sometimes we really do need new words, I call the gap apraxis. The medical term apraxia means a form of paralysis, an inability to carry out intention. That fits: it's not that you've seen the gap between your walk and your talk and are shrugging it off; it's that something's gone wrong and you can't see the gap.

All of us practicing Christians "do" apraxis because that's what we are: practicing, not perfect. The only difference between one and the next is how big the gap is and how determined one's ignorance of it is. Some Christians veer toward perfectionism, constantly doing the left hand/right hand match; this can lead either to a neurotic sort of perpetually chewing your own wrists or, if you take the healthier route, to the notion that maybe you're the sort of sinner Christ died for and you'd better accept both that fact and his redemption. Not one of us doesn't have a Shadow—a dragon peeking over the shoulder that we really don't like to look at, but that people who are face-to-face with us can see. And the whole business of becoming spiritually grown-up depends on facing that dragon, accepting that it really does belong to you, and figuring out what you're going to do about it.

But what do you do with the really egregious cases—say, the secret-police torturer who devoutly attends Mass every single Sunday and saint's day, without exception, or the officer who's such a good family man and who orders the slaughter of a whole village, men, women, and children? What about the husband who claims to love his wife, but who screams abuse at her and beats her up—and then snaps back to normal as though nothing had happened? What of the woman who claims to be truthful and loving but who leaves a trail of emotional havoc in her wake, quite genuinely without any knowledge of what she's done? What about the teachers in Indian residential schools who systematically violated dozens of children and never could figure out that they'd done anything really wrong? What about these two priests, sworn before God and the bishop to the service of a Lord who proclaimed God's love, who posted rank malevolence on the Internet? That's what Max and I wondered about. How can you grow a dragon that size and be so completely unaware that it exists?

As Max and I were standing at his front door one afternoon trying, for the tenth time at least, to figure what the hell was going on here, I found myself getting jumped by a very big metaphor. I am not responsible for metaphors like this; I do not make them up. They sneak up on me from God alone knows where. I had a sort of vision, of a man sitting in a chair, focusing on a tray propped across the arms of the chair. The tray held tiles, the inch-square glazed type, and some of the tiles were bright and some were dark and some were in between.

As I watched, he carefully picked out and removed all the very dark tiles and put them on a small table, to his right and behind him, out of sight, and rearranged all the remaining tiles to fill in the gaps. But now, some of the less dark tiles offended him, so he picked them out and put them on the table too, and rearranged the remainder. He went through this several times, gradually getting rid of all the shadowy tiles, until all that were left for him to look at were the brightest and most glowing tiles. He would not or could not turn his head and see the table with dark tiles behind him. But I could see it, and as I watched, I could see all those dark tiles starting to fuse and take on a new shape, one that shim-mied and wobbled and seemed to be growing into something liv-ing. And I felt afraid.

It made sense now. If you can't afford to have negative thoughts or emotions—if they make you feel too ashamed or too afraid of being punished, or if they threaten to sink you altogether—you put them off to one side and behind you, so that you won't have to look at them. And you keep doing that until what you can see of yourself looks okay—until you can feel good about yourself, self-satisfied, or at least less frightened and anxious. Problem is, the stuff that you've rejected hasn't gone away, because it's part of you. That pile of darkness behind you turns into a large dragonish be-ing that you can't see but that looks over your shoulder at the world before you, seeing it through a miasma of bitter unlove, frightening and hurting the people it fronts, and you can't figure out what's gotten into them—you were just playing around a little, nothing serious, you didn't mean it the way they took it.

Maybe you suspect there might be something there, something unmanageable and unnerving, so you redouble your efforts to focus on the bright tiles on your tray, humming to yourself quite loudly, so as to drown out the noises coming from behind you that you don't want to listen to. But it's such hard work . . . I remembered people I knew who seemed seriously Jekyll-and-Hyde-ish, and I started to understand the sheer effort involved in maintaining that separation. All of a sudden, I could see why it paralyzed them and left them exhausted and often depressed. It takes one hell of a lot of work to maintain invincible self-ignorance in this world.

Or maybe we find it simpler to hand off all that darkness to someone else to carry. Maybe that's where the sort of craziness in those posts was coming from. . . . The J-and-H people I knew were, without exception, both extremely nice people *and* extremely judgmental ones, with a knack for vindictiveness and "out"-grouping—like the decent, friendly townspeople in Shirley Jackson's story "The Lottery." We scapegoat because it's easier to hand off our own evil to someone else than it is to take it, look at it, and accept its ugliness as our own. It's less work than fighting it off.

I've done this myself. In my old life, anger was something I couldn't afford: being angry or uppity was the one thing that would, for sure, make the abuse flow like lava down a hillside. Anger was extremely dangerous stuff. Besides, I was only valuable for being a loving, accepting, forgiving sort of person: that was the carrot. But I also had good reasons for being angry; I should have been confronting, not forgiving. What do you do with the anger you can't afford to feel or express? I took some of it into myself, where it turned into a toxic strain of self-blame and self-doubt—a classic woman's tactic. And the rest I stacked behind me and off to one side, where I didn't have to look at it and could forget about it. I did forget about it, honestly; I had no idea it was there. But those who looked me in the face could see it, and they reported it back to me, and I was shocked and defensive. Only when life slowly got safe again and normalcy looked to be finally within grasp could I afford to feel anger again. And then, because I knew it was right and had the confidence to do so, I could reach behind me, pick up those dark tiles from the quivering mass, and put them back on my own tray of tiles, where I can keep an eye on them.

Maybe this is what a reasonable sense of sin is really about: not hating yourself, not judging and condemning yourself, but understanding that you do have those tiles on your tray and you'd better keep them there, under your eye, managing them properly, rather than letting them get up to God knows what behind your back. I know now that, as well as a capacity for anger, I have a strongly judgmental streak; if I admit this and accept that it's something I have to manage, then maybe that streak will do others and me less harm. The problem is when I claim to be a totally nonjudgmental person; then I drive the people around me nuts because my talk is wildly out of whack with my walk, and my judgmentalism starts to nip and claw innocent bystanders because I'm pretending that I have nothing to do with it—rather like the owner of a large dog who doesn't keep the animal leashed.

Integrity is oneness: the fusion of walk and talk, the acceptance of our own inner darkness; the determined acceptance of reality, however unappealing it sometimes is. This tray-of-tiles business, like hypocrisy, is the opposite of integrity. The hypocrite separates this world into Theory and Practice and says that the two can exist side by side, without fusion; he or she accepts the dualism and sees no problem there. The man with the tray of tiles is different. He's found a way of being at one with himself by chucking out all the parts he doesn't like and putting them where he doesn't have to acknowledge them. And I suppose it does make for a strange sort of integrity: all the tiles on the tray were uniformly bright and handsome.

But it won't work. I don't know how long you can manage to keep up the act, but sooner or later, it must collapse, if for no other reason than sheer exhaustion. It's terribly, terribly tiring to defend yourself against self-knowledge; you must become increasingly rigid—a smaller and smaller person, more bitterly defended. I don't envy the man with the tray of tiles. Yes, he bought himself a certain peace, but at what cost?

Better, I think, to keep all the tiles you've got and to see what you can make with and of them. All of us are such a mixed lot that any one of us can afford to be that way. There's no point pretending to God anyway. He already knows.

# WATERCOLORS

The package came via UPS, a flattish rectangular box. She recognized the return address immediately: what the hell? She'd talked to Annie only a couple of weeks back, and she hadn't mentioned that she was sending anything. Puzzled, she took a knife to the parcel's taped ends, pulling out the packing, a paper-wrapped something (biggish book? no; too light), and a note. Putting the wrapped thing down, she opened the note first. "Found this among Tom's things. I didn't have the least idea what was in it—think these must be yours??? He'd never mentioned them. Can't think who else they'd belong to. Love, Annie."

She'd never seen the portfolio before, she was sure of that. It was a grayish leather business-type thing with a zipper, no ties, a little larger than letter size, maybe twelve by sixteen inches, clearly of good quality, not new. She felt strangely frightened: what did it hold? She and her brother had ended up close, and she had been with him and Annie when he died; but there was that time long ago, nearly ten years of a breach so total it seemed unmendable. They never spoke of that time. Was this something from back then? She lived, always, with the fear that something would happen to drag her back there, and so she disliked surprises. I'll open it after lunch, she told herself. And then: no, better get it over with.

The zipper slipped open smoothly, and she carried the portfolio over to her kitchen table, clearing away the newspaper and setting the portfolio down open. It held a sheaf of artist's drawing paper, heavy, deckle-edged, slightly textured. She turned over the first leaf and froze.

Some things you lose so thoroughly, you can't remember ever having had them.

Oh yes, she knew this drawing. She knew them all. She had forgotten, for more than twenty-five years, that they had ever existed. Forgotten be damned; she had wiped them out of memory so completely that there wasn't even a hint of a vacancy, of a place they'd ever occupied. But she knew them. Of course she knew them. They were a dozen or so pen-and-ink drawings and watercolor sketches of plants and flowers, the drawings crisp and exact, the watercolors surprisingly strong, yet transparent. She had sent them to him in desperation the summer she turned twenty-one.

The kitchen closed down around her, shrinking to the size of

a big cleaning closet, and the light darkened, and she sat unmov-
ing, unseeing, her fingertips lying lightly on the edge of the
stacked drawings, and she herself was elsewhere . . . back in the
lab, looking at a specimen of *Vaccinium uliginosum* (that's bog bil-
berry) and meticulously measuring and sketching it. She'd had to
take biology in college—it was a required course. She'd feared it
at first, being an artsy type with that arts-student belief that science was deeply, mystifyingly boring. But then she'd discovered
looking into microscopes and had tumbled head over heels in love:
a whole new sea to troll in . . . Her lab instructor found, for the
first time, a student who could actually *interpret* a paramecium. The
prof, a botanist, hired her to draw for him, illustrations for his taxonomy of the genus *Vaccinium*—blueberries and cranberries and
their close relatives, lovely things, a pleasure to work with.

That summer, she'd stayed in the city instead of going home,
subletting a grotty apartment, living poor, sketching and painting
type specimens for him. It was work she loved. But even then the
darkness was closing around her: some days she could work and
some days it was a major achievement just to get her shoes tied.
Out of a kindness he could not articulate, and so she never really
knew about it, the botanist kept her tiny stipend going, pretending she was still working. And so she was, but not for him: she
could no longer manage even that little contact. She was sick, she
knew it, and she was so shamed by her sickness that she could deal
only with people who were at or below her own level. That in
turn drew her further down. And so it went.

She went on drawing and painting that endless, gritty summer,
not the type specimens—the prof had those, of course—but ordi-

nary plants that caught her wavering fancy, plants stolen from parks or gardens, weeds she'd found in the corner of gray parking lots or springing from cracks in the concrete. She had brought them home and put them in water on a table on the tiny apartment balcony, where the light was better. As she drew precisely in india ink or meticulously layered on watercolors, she found that she could push the darkness away, at least sometimes, at least for a few minutes: she could lose herself. And lost was the best she could manage.

Just before the darkness closed over her, sensing she was going under and wanting to salvage these beloveds, like a drowning parent pushing a child to safety, she'd sent her drawings off to Tom. His scrawled note acknowledging them and saying what he thought of them had been the last thing before she finally crashed. She had no intention of remembering what followed, ever.

But now she was middleaged, respectable, prosperous, sane, chaste, clean, and balanced: calmly and contentedly married; mother to two sometimes difficult but promising, lively teenaged daughters; a highly respected freelance graphic designer with more clients than she wanted and much too little time. They had a light, pleasant, airy house in a subdivision so new that everything was still under warranty. She spent her days laying out text, importing graphics, pondering typefaces and papers and color schemes, raking over the work again and again until it was exquisitely balanced, the spacing perfect—all done by computer (Quark on a Mac platform). She had not picked up a paintbrush, except the big housepainting type, for decades, and the only pens she now owned were ballpoints and one dressy fountain pen for special notes, always dry. The closest she ever got to nature these days was a walk in the park. That was then. Now was now. And now was so much better than then . . .

She put the drawings away and went downstairs to her base-ment office: she had a brochure to lay out for a trade show, ad-vertising computer peripherals, routine stuff, but she couldn't concentrate. Settling down at the Mac, she pulled up the file and studied it, finding it disgustingly flat. Almost randomly, she moved a graphic a touch further up the page, and the computer froze: oh shit, crashed again. Frustrated, suddenly flapping her hands, she got up and moved around her office, picking up what small mild disorder there was: she needed everything tidy, or she found her-self getting anxious . . .

. . . and memory seized her again. *Oh God, not memory. Stop it!* She was back in her second-year watercolors class, drawing a still life, a bowl of apples set on a table strewn with chrysanthemums and the preserved corpse of a red squirrel. She'd already spent hours after class, because watercolors took her so long. She had painted each fleck on each apple, each petal on each chrysanthe-mum, carefully overpainting, and was now meticulously rendering squirrel fur one microstroke at a time. The other students, mean-while, were rioting in happy abstraction, working fast, tossing on colors boldly, blurrily, and with sublime confidence. It would take them one-tenth of the time it took her, and they'd give her hell for being so literal-minded, so fussy. Cheap picture-postcard stuff, they said; showed an obvious lack of imagination. You're not supposed to *photograph* the goddam squirrel; you're supposed to *interpret* the thing. Crowding around, they analyzed her emotional/creative constipation, ripping her open with what they saw as honesty. The loudest was the boy she thought she was in love with and who had taken her to bed just once before dropping her for a dark-haired flautist. Shrinking away, she fled, taking her unfinished drawing with her. On her knees behind the student union, she ripped it up into the smallest pieces she could. That afternoon, she went to the registrar's office, dropped her art classes, and changed her major to English. After that, she kept her drawing to herself. Except in botany, where they wanted her kind of accuracy and creative imagination wasn't an issue.

And then Tom, her own brother: saying something along the same lines when she'd trusted him with these drawings. He said that they were well enough, but she needed to stretch. He hadn't meant it as a betrayal; she knew that even at the time. But it was a mild and appropriate rap of the knuckles falling on top of a fracture, and the pain was such that she was walking into walls. Looking at the drawings now, she could see both sides. They *were* meticulous, beautifully drawn—God, I did have draftsmanship, didn't I? The watercolors managed that tricky line between depth and transparency; she was pleased to find that she'd had that knack. They were first-rate student art. But only student art— rather like a writer describing something in exquisite detail, but without conveying the meaning of it. Tom had been right. It was just that, at that time, his rightness was about the last thing she'd needed.

Memory flooded her, incontinent, uncontrollable. A sketchbook she'd owned, bound in heavy cardboard with a splendid Chinese-red cover, marked up by coffee rings. What had become of that book? She'd filled it with drawings; walked with it under her arm, trolling for interesting stuff, stopping whenever she found something, to make a quick sketch. There had been bigger pieces, now she remembered them: bigger watercolors built up with painstaking love, rolled carefully in tubes for storage: a streetscape with dark trees forming a green tunnel; an abandoned Georgian brick house; a Scotch pine with the light coming sideways from the west, making the bark a rich sienna brocade. Other pieces, maybe a couple of dozen in all, some dating back to high school. All gone, irretrievable, and suddenly she was swamped by overwhelming grief, as she might feel for a child miscarried—grief for those pictures, and for her younger self. She'd had them when she slipped into the darkness; when she'd finally woken up in the white room, detoxed, cleaned up, emaciated, numb, and terribly vacant, she had been empty-handed. Had she burned them in a drunken fury? Had she traded them for hash or speed? Had they been lost as she moved from one dump to another? She had no real memories of that time, only the odd spot or flash in the blackness, and no memory that she wanted back. Sometimes she still got flashbacks, or dreams that left her feeling spent, shaky, and desolate. *Four whole years. I don't know what I did or who I fucked or what I took.* It did not occur to her that, for the first time, she was thinking of the dark time with pity, not terror.

Could she get them all back in mind, if she tried? Without

knowing, she'd drifted back to the portfolio in the kitchen. She picked up one of the drawings—it was a dandelion like a sunburst—and sniffed; it was faintly musty, and she saw traces of foxing at the edges.

She closed her eyes involuntarily and found herself looking at a peony, painted on the back of her eyelids. It was a splendidly blowsy peony, trembling on the verge of vulgarity, a deep formal rose-pink. *I had a dress that color when I was eighteen; whatever became of it?* It was a peony like a fat middle-aged woman dressed splendidly in flowing reds and teals and purples, shaking her gray-black curls back and eyeballing the world in knowledge, love, and deep amusement. She wanted more than anything else in the world to paint that peony. Right now. It was like being in labor and being told not to push: impossible to stop or go back.

The thought panicked her. *I can't. I don't have any materials.* Armstrong's, her mind said back to her. She hadn't been there for years, not since the kids were little; she'd taken them there for watercolor sets and had had to leave fast, dragging them crying behind her, fleeing from the faint unmistakable odor of sketch pads and pastels, new canvas and turps. *I want a wooden pen with changeable nibs, charcoal, india ink. I want very, very fine brushes.* She'd never had the money for really good brushes. Now she did. What stopped her was fear. *I've forgotten how.* It will come back, it will. The fear tightened her chest, making her heart yammer; she was breathing fast and short. *Oh, Tom, what have you done?*

That peony. It *needed* her. It wanted to be done like a seventeenth-century botanical print; her graphics knowledge stood at her shoulder, choosing the background and selecting type for a caption, something deflating the seriousness of the form in a historically appropriate font. *This time, if anyone's going to mock my stuff, it's going to be me. That'll keep me honest.*

Honesty. I have been like a suburban lawn for ages, she thought: trimmed back, uniform, because I was so afraid of chaos. But lawn grass can't fruit; it's never allowed to grow that far. It's a mere monoculture, requiring an enormous investment in time, chemicals, water, just to be a flat and featureless carpet. She saw long grass growing in a ditch, the graceful panicles. If I want to bear anything, I have to get a little shaggy. She was still afraid, but now with a tingle of excitement. *God, it's been so dull for so long.*

*But what have I got to say? And why would anyone want to hear it?* She could hear a voice in her mind, the voice of a casually cruel young man saying *Christ, how banal.* Well, maybe one of the advantages of being middle-aged is that you know life *is* banal. I'm past the age of Mozart and Byron. There's nothing truly new under the sun; it's only what you do with it.

She glanced at the kitchen clock. If she hurried, she could get to Armstrong's and pick up a few basics and be back in time to start supper. She shrugged on a jacket and found her car keys, knowing she would not hurry.

# THE CLUB

It was a crisp, clear April morning. Susan had just come into her office after a Chamber of Commerce business break-fast, hung up her coat, got water from the bathroom, and started the usual pot of coffee. It looked to be a good morning, another good day in a good and happy life. She loved her handsome old office building and her job; she liked her colleagues and felt very much a part of the neighborhood. This was where normal was: her church up the street, the Y where she showered and changed after biking in each morning, the library she read in, the credit of-fice in the next-door federal building, where she and the tellers chatted as she did her banking. Some people think of downtown as impersonal or cold. She knew it as her community. She knew the faces.

This fine spring morning, she stood by her office window, smelling the fresh brew and admiring a little crystal cross that hung in her office window over the coffeemaker. Then she took her fresh coffee to the door of her office and stood for a moment, chatting with a colleague: was her 9 A.M. client going to show or not? And then, out of nowhere, the world abruptly thundered, and the whole building shook so hard that they both fell down, and all the windows blew in. And then Susan's office fell on top of her, smashed to bits.

She wrote it all out afterward, and her narrative has the calm, clear affectlessness of deep shock: how she got to her feet, noticing mildly that the buttons had been blown off her suit and she'd lost her shoes; how she and the others walked quite calmly down the stairs and out of the building; how orderly everybody was. She wasn't surprised to see them carrying out small limp children; she knew that there were day-care centers in both the federal building and the nearby Y. She didn't notice that she was covered in blood, but others did and cared for her. There was so much kindness. She felt cold; a total stranger wrapped her in a dark blue sweater. She watched a friend almost bleed to death, holding her hand (the friend survived).

And then she was in the hospital, and they were giving her little pinpricks of local anesthetic while they cleaned her up and sutured away, because her poor shattered office had stuck her full as a pincushion with plaster shards and broken glass. She has three and a half feet of stitching on the normally visible parts of her hide, and that's not counting the ropes of scar tissue up and down her back. The explosion half tore her ear off. It took weeks for all the bits of glass to work their way out of her flesh.

There were other scars too. The loss of health, independence, vitality—this comes hard to a vigorous young woman, one who'd always been proud of her ability to stand on her own two feet and do for others instead of having others do for her. Those nice tellers she'd chatted with at the credit union: half were dead. She, Susan, had survived; she met and talked to the parents of another Susan, who hadn't. And she knew that she would have died herself if she hadn't moved away from her window. It was that close.

Now, suddenly, she had to deal with that huge unmanageable lump: just what *do* we do with Evil? For that question wasn't going to be shelved, not this time, and facile answers wouldn't work. Two young men had parked that truck full of homemade explosive outside the Murrah Building. They knew about that day-care center, and they chose to go ahead regardless. Most likely they didn't see those children or the workers in that building and surrounding buildings as people at all. They saw them as stick figures, not worth thinking about—Lego minifigures, clothespin dolls, mere carbon units. That their bomb would kill so many, cause such havoc and suffering, mattered no more to the bombers than snapping a Popsicle stick between the fingers. None of it was really *real*. The mark of the narcissist . . .

That's always what Evil is really about—denying the reality of what we've done and what we've inflicted on others, refusing to

71

see them as properly human, treating them as things, no more sig-nificant than the grass to be mown when the lawn gets too shaggy. Maybe Evil has no real independent existence; maybe it's only a fragment of who each of us is. I've heard a convincing case for that. I'm sure that Evil exists; it's only a question of where—on its own, or in us all, or both. But I'm convinced of one thing: not only is it banal, but Evil has all the creativity, vitality, imagination, understanding, foresight, and analytical power of your average stunned night crawler. It's always unproductive and it's usually as dumb as a sack of hammers. If Evil has any energy or intelligence, it's because we've lent it ours.

Susan had to wrestle with the big question of forgiveness too—not in the sense of letting those responsible off the hook; later she testified at one of their sentencing trials. But some of the victims stayed stuck in that one tearing moment, frozen in grief and anger, unable to move, and that she would not do. The bombing marked her deeply, body and soul; it also set her off on a long journey. "I went to work and got blown up. Other people went to work, and life will never be the same again. Children went to day care and died." *So: now what am I going to make of it all?*

She wrote:

*A few days after the bombing, on my way home from the hospital to the friends who would take care of me, I stopped for a moment to see my buddies at the State Chamber of Commerce. Fran greeted me with the words that I was absolutely the most beautiful sight she had seen, when I felt at my most unlovely. Dick knelt in front of me, kissed my hands, and as a Vietnam combat veteran, welcomed me to the trauma club.*

Susan knew that her normal was gone; she could never get back what she'd lost in that split second when the world exploded. She knew that she'd have to build a new normal from scratch—new habits, new spaces, new community—instead of staying frozen, looking back at what she had lost. She could help in the struggle to set her church building to rights, but it's not the church it was before, and she is not the woman who worshipped there before. In this life, those yards of scars will always be on her hide, just as the face of her town will never be as it was. But there was this comfort: that she belonged to a whole secret society that knew exactly how it felt, and that could offer love.

People join the club through all sorts of experiences, some obvious, some not. For very many, it's not one huge big horror; it's a whole succession of small big horrors, one intolerable thing after another that you have to tolerate because you have absolutely no choice in the matter. I don't know how the Vietnam vets get by, the ones who had it real bad. How do they get through the day, living with the flashbacks, the sense of helplessness, the anxiety, the fits of rage?—all the woundedness of a soul who should never have seen this shit, never been forced into this situation. Some must have found it easier to die, literally or in spirit; others snapped and went into darkness and did things that they probably will never be able to remember, because some things you just can't handle.

For still others, it's just one damn thing after another: a friend's death after a bankruptcy after a parent's severe illness after a cancer scare after a child going off the rails after a job downsizing, until the whole world just looks like one door slamming after another. You might go under; or you might deny that anything's wrong at all. Or you might give up and join the club.

But for every big-bang trauma, there's probably another case that doesn't make any noise at all, other than the occasional smashed dish or shouting match and a whole lot of quiet sobbing. Oh, there may be the occasional explosion, enough to keep you scared and wary and to cause long-term changes to your adrenaline levels, but that's not how the real harm happens. Instead, it comes on so slowly that you don't even realize what's happening. It's apt to be a series of small things, little surrenders, compromises that seemed not so bad at the time; it's only looking back that you see how they all added up. At the time, it all seemed so trivial that you never thought to challenge what was happening, and besides, as time went on, you lost your energy and confidence, one nibble at a time. That's when the evil becomes the wallpaper of your life, stuff you don't even really notice anymore because you're so used to it. It's now normal, and you no longer think to question it. You can be blown up, or you can die of repeated wounds. Or you can be chilled to death almost without knowing it at all.

However it happened, big or small, loud or quiet, you find yourself joining the club. At least your fellow members are apt to understand and to welcome you with open arms. In the club, people don't compare and dismiss; they are uninterested in the hierarchy of suffering ("My pain is bigger'n your pain!"). They respect each other's experience too much for that. They know that there are scars and scars, and some you wear on the outside, like Susan, and others you wear on the inside, also like Susan. They know that enough small wounds over enough time leave just as many yards of stitches. They don't need you to be whole and fully functional and just fine. It almost doesn't matter where you are, because they've been through equivalent landscapes—and you may learn to your humility that some have been through much, much worse.

Susan says, "The funny thing is that you can almost tell when meeting someone whether or not they have gone through the horrible initiation rites. . . . People who have been initiated into the trauma club are unafraid to face someone else's pain." Their response to it is simply to put their arms out, because they know that's what they needed—to have that warm blue sweater wrapped about their bleeding shoulders, to be cared for by the compassion of strangers. But members don't push and they don't ask questions and they don't demand to see the stitches, because they also remember how that felt.

They know the secondary hurts. They know the deep shame of having to deal with fits of rage or anxiety that pop up like sudden zits on a teenaged brow. They know how it feels to live with physical disabilities in a culture that unsexes and depersonalizes the ill—how to live with obvious scarring in a world that pays thousands of dollars to airbrush Michelle Pfeiffer's face for a magazine cover shot. They know just how it feels to be stared at in an airport, how to handle the dumb comments: "Are you a Vietnam vet? Well, you know, you folks just overreacted." "You say you lived for years with spousal abuse? Well, what stopped you from leaving?" "There's nothing to stop losers like that Harry from going out and getting a job, even if he did go through a tough time. Sitting around all day, claiming he's depressed. Huh." Sightseers in dark glasses stop by the site of the Murrah Building and take snapshots of each other, smiling and waving for the camera. And, of course, there's the stubborn universal human instinctive belief that bad luck must be self-inflicted and might possibly be contagious—that it's better to avoid the walking wounded and hang out with the lucky, beautiful, and fortunate, because you have to be careful about what might rub off on you. That's one good thing about being in the trauma club. You know what bullshit that is, and so do the people who have put their arms around you.

Membership does bring hard-earned benefits. For example, sometimes you gain a certain clarity; you begin to have some understanding of just how many beans make five, although you may find yourself losing the need to jump up and down on people who think beans are confusing. Sometimes you find yourself being wept upon by that poor bruised princess, forced to put up with that horrid pea under all the feather beds. Being a member of the club, you can say, with some sympathy (because pain is still pain and it hurts), but also with authority: "Child, I'm sure that pea was miserable and you're feeling sore all over, but please stop calling it deeply traumatic; it isn't, it's just part of the way life is. Most people sleep on the cold bare ground. Remember that and be grateful."

But the chief glory of joining the trauma club is that it takes you into deserts where you have never been, and it lets you find the fruits and the sudden pools of fresh water. For Jesus had it right: blessed are the uncertain, blessed are those that mourn, blessed are the poor. Not because suffering is a good thing in and of itself, but because it does tend to clear the decks.

*S*o there you are, newly inducted into the club, standing at the edge of the wilderness in your undershorts or slip, shivering and bewildered, still in shock, perhaps, looking into no future that you'd ever dreamed of imagining. If you had any notion that you could control your circumstances, put it down right here. That, like so many other things, has been blown off and away from you like the buttons from Susan's suit jacket.

You must take the desert on its own terms and adapt to it, living with and through it as Moses and his people did for forty years; as Jesus did for forty days, wrestling with the darker sides of being human. You'll learn very quickly that much of what you thought important isn't. Networking doesn't work here; power plays are of no conceivable interest. Career moves—what career? Why would that matter? All the clichés that used to entice, notions of being faster and shrewder and more fashionable than your peers—these shrivel and curl up like withered chiles. They're as useful in the desert as a silver-plated cake plate.

But other things, things that you took for granted or didn't think important, start becoming all-consuming: love, honesty, family, community, vulnerability, your own need to give and accept care, your essential powerlessness, that sense that someone's there, looking after you. You think about things that you'd never thought of before: who am I, really? who's my God? why did all this happen? and what am I going to make of it all?

Look around you. You are walking on known trails that other pilgrims have taken. They knew where to find the fruit and springs of fresh water that can sustain you even through a long, long journey. And some of them are with you now, other members of the club. They know you; they know to count up from the bottom, not down from the top. Some days, you're almost normal. Some days, you aren't. Some days, with luck and hard work, you may just about manage to get your shoes tied, and that's true victory. And they know that too.

What you carry into the desert is your soul, the one and only thing you can take on this journey. When you reach the other side—and you may not; you may choose to stay here, as many do—you'll find that that soul has changed. Its priorities are different. It knows what gold is real and what's just pretty pyrite. It holds tight to love, and to it the world is so very full of beauty, as well as suffering.

Susan writes of living *vita brevis*—living with the knowledge that life is brief.

*To live* vita brevis *means to count as precious the days remaining. You do not know when the end will come. We just went to work that morning. 169 people did not come home that evening, and for count-*

*less others, life will never ever be the same. Ever. I don't have time to waste. It has made a difference to how I order my work and my personal life. Interesting, because I find myself wanting every minute at work to make a difference, yet on a personal level, "wasting time" with family and friends seems more important than anything else.*

*. . . I think of some of the profound tender acts shown to me that will stay with me and affect my relationship with that person forever. To be the recipient of that tender act sometimes causes me to perform a tender act with another person in another kind of trauma, and that interconnectedness plays on.*

And that's the final victory: that Evil can push a soul not off the edge, but into something deeper and holier than we could ever ask or imagine.

# THE SORROW OF NARCISSA

No touch of his could leave the least print upon her. If he tried to hold her lovingly, she'd accept his affection for a moment, amused but unmoved, and then go back to whatever she'd been doing, as though she'd put what she really cared about on hold for him, purely as a favor, but without any material interest. When, much later and to his utter astonishment, he did find love, he was almost stunned to learn that it mattered to his lover that he put his arms around her; that something in her uncurled and bloomed when he did that. He was that used to making no difference at all.

It had been this way from the first moment their infatuation faded, not long after the wedding. At first he thought that all would come right again with time, work, and patience, and he was ready to give it everything he had. After that failed to change anything, he thought for a while that it was simply a marriage gone wrong, and that she'd be happy and free without him, able to find someone she could love. It happens in marriages sometimes: one party or both find that it was a mistake, and sadly they bring things to an end. Periodically he offered to leave, but she said no, she wanted him to stay; she needed him—for what, he never did understand. Those were the times that she'd cling to him, pouring out all the warmth he'd missed so badly, lying childlike and quiet in his arms, so that each time he came away hopeful that somehow it would all work out. He still loved her, and he had promised before God. He hoped that if he loved her carefully enough, thoughtfully enough, with sufficient patience and devotion, maybe someday he'd be able to break through to whoever was inside her. But that wasn't working either.

It began to eat at him, this sense of having failed her somehow, in ways he couldn't understand. She made him feel like such a fool, so clumsy, so insensitive, thick as a brick. She claimed to be a simple, uncomplicated soul: why did he have so little sense of what she was really like? She was so honest and transparent; if he couldn't really understand her, it obviously was his problem, not hers. He had a humble notion of his own solid intelligence, compared with her dancing, impish brilliance. It was easier to see himself as all wrong than it was to question her rightness.

Still seeking the insight he so clearly lacked, he bought and read psychology texts, books on family relations, studying system after system, and each made sense in its way, some more than others. And clearly he had learned something, for he found himself being a better manager at work—even getting a reputation around his company for his people skills and insight. That helped him stay afloat. But no system he came across made any sense of her. When he compared her with all the models, she didn't match at all. She was charming, remote, elusive, unreachable, and unlike any other. She was proud of that, and so was he; it made her special.

They almost never disagreed. It seemed easier not to challenge her, somehow—easier to go along with her choices, even when he didn't entirely like them. He didn't know how it had happened, but he found himself saying over and over, "Doesn't matter to me—whatever you'd like." He no longer questioned her right to decide where they'd go for his birthday dinner out. And he'd learned, long since, not to get angry with her. The few times he had, she would cry heartbrokenly until he felt horrible, and then she'd confront him with how controlling and abusive he was being, and it would come up over and over again, for months afterward, no matter how much he apologized—but nothing would really change. He learned to step very, very carefully around her; he never quite knew what would set her off, and that too made him feel thick as a brick.

But sometimes, for no apparent reason, she would open her lovely mouth in all apparent innocence and drop a comment that stunned him with its sheer cruelty, and he would walk away reeling, wondering what he had done or said or been, that she should hate him so ferociously. Then she'd meet him at the dinner table half an hour later, sunny and charming, as though nothing whatsoever had happened. If he tried to bring the matter up, she said that she'd only wanted to help him; everything she said, she said in kindness and love. He just had to learn to accept friendly criticism, which is all she'd intended. She should have remembered that he couldn't deal with any negative feedback—but he really should, as an adult, toughen up just a little. And she would laugh and pat his face and turn the conversation to something more interesting.

Once—only once in all those years—he came to her, sat down next to her as she read her magazine on the sofa, and took her hand and said that he wished they could be truly close. He spoke to her as soul to soul, open and vulnerable, offering up his love as an act of trust, asking her trust in return. She heard him out politely, turned away from his direct and questing look, and said, in that kind, warm voice of hers, with just a hint of chuckle, "I've always said that with me, what you see is what you get. I'm sorry if you think I'm not good enough for you, but I do my best—I wish you'd give me just a little credit for that!" And then she turned back to her magazine. He sat transfixed, a long glass shard punched through his heart; the pain was so intense that for a long moment he could not move at all. And then he got up and went to the kitchen and fixed himself a drink. He never brought the matter up again.

If he'd been less of a healthy person, probably he would have gone under, like the blank-faced men he knew who were stuck in loveless or bitter marriages that they felt they could not leave. Something dies, and the infection from the rot of it spreads into the soul, leaving a funny sort of necrosis. But he had had the taste of love in childhood; he knew that it existed and what it felt like. Love *was*. He knew the taste of it. Under his growing self-blame, under the spreading paralysis that seemed to have hold of him, he treasured a hidden sense of self. In his loneliness, he started to spend more time with that self, drawing away from her. But strangely, he also found himself spending time with some other-ness outside himself and the whole situation: there was a Something there, and it was with him in ways he didn't understand either, but this nonunderstanding wasn't a failure; it was perfectly fine. He could trust it. He could go back to his younger self, the boy who'd been so full of hope, all those years ago, and the Something would be with him. He had not always been alone. He was not alone now.

As he began to draw away, a little at a time, they entered a long period of unstated struggle, some tussle that neither of them voiced, about who was going to own his soul, her or him, or maybe that Something. There was a single moment at which things underwent a tiny, radical shift, like a bump so small you barely notice it, the result of some quiet earthquake that leaves things totally rearranged. They had been having one of their long, wavering, difficult-to-sustain discussions over after-dinner coffee, and he realized for the first time that she was watching herself in the ornamental mirror of the old oak sideboard: her face might be turned in his direction, but her eyes kept flicking away to her own reflection. Later, they made love for the first time in many weeks, and again, when they were eye-to-eye, he wondered if she was indeed looking lovingly at him, as he'd always thought and desired, or if in fact all she saw in his eyes was the tiny image of her own face.

After that, his observations came unbidden, thick and fast. He began to see that she always seemed to be watching herself, keeping a mostly approving eye on her own performance, with a secret satisfied little smile. He was idly rummaging through a box of photos one evening and came across one that he'd taken of her during a trip they'd made to Pakistan. She'd visited a girls' school and made a generous donation. The photo showed her white, slim, and lovely in a waist-high sea of children: their dark faces turned up, hands reaching toward her, huge smiles all aimed in her direction—all these uniformed little girls adoring her, and there she was with that same small secret smile, drinking in their worship with greedy little sips. It made him wonder.

Now that he saw that, he also began to see other ways in which she just didn't add up. Her much-vaunted kindness, for example. They had both been so proud of how much she gave to those in need. They could afford philanthropy, and she loved being a philanthropist. Now he began to note that whenever a recipient of her generosity turned too independent, she would get upset or coldly dismissive and drop that person like a hot rock. He didn't want to see it, but he had no choice.

The real shock came the first time they had one of their rare quarrels. It was over one of her protégées; she'd dropped the person, cut off her badly needed help, because the woman wouldn't take her advice about raising her children. The woman had called him, desperate and crying, and he'd promised to bring the matter up. He did, after dinner one day; she turned cold and dismissive, but for once, keeping his promise, he persisted, pushing her hard. Turning on him, she hissed out one of her poisonous little observations, a quick burst of such rage and hatred and sheer spite, as corrosive as concentrated acid. In an instant, she was back to her calm and smiling self, as though nothing had happened.

But this time something was different. Just as she seemed always to be watching herself, so now a part of him stood aside from his anger and hurt and watched the two of them. And for the first time, he saw, really *saw*, that she had literally no idea of what she'd said—not the slightest inkling that her comment could really hurt him, or that there was any unkindness in her words. She genuinely believed that she'd "spoken the truth in love" for his own sake, but her belief had no relation at all to the reality of what she'd said. It wasn't pretense; it was quite genuine—a division as deep and final as a crack in the universe. Or no—it was like color blindness or tone deafness or a nonexistent sense of smell. She could not hear her own words. In all honesty, she just couldn't get it.

That was the breaking moment. His anger poofed out abruptly, like a blown-out candle, and he found himself looking at her with a strange new sobriety. He knew, with a certainty that came from outside himself, that this could not go on: that if something didn't break, he was going to die. At the same time, he felt like a man who had twisted himself sideways into knots of cramping pain in order to conform to what she wanted of him, and he found himself inwardly straightening up, shaking out his limbs and stretching, wondering at the sense of space and air and health. *I am not stupid:* he knew this quite suddenly. If she had this failing, this blank imperception, then the problem was not entirely his. It might be at least partially hers as well.

The conversation stopped abruptly. She was looking at him strangely, almost fearfully. He pushed back his chair and got up, turning his back on her, and went out on the side porch. He had no idea whether she tried to come after him, and he didn't care. It was a summer night, cool and dank after rain, but the fireflies were out and he watched their flickering, sitting on the porch steps: a man apparently elsewhere, totally blank, eyes open but unseeing. His mind felt entirely empty.

He felt his field of vision constrict, and in the center of that narrowed darkness he saw a bright image growing, becoming more focused. There was an old-fashioned wood-framed standing full-length mirror, and before the mirror there sat a very small child, hardly more than a toddler, a girl of maybe two or three. He knew, for he could feel her mind, that she was utterly alone, sad and frightened. She was hungry and had wet herself. She was much too little to be left by herself like this; where were the adults? She called and cried and even screamed, turning brick red, but no one came. In the end she gave up and got unsteadily to her feet, wiping her blubbery nose on the hem of her skirt.

She turned to the mirror and laid her small warm palms on the cold glass palms of the child facing her, looking into that child's chubby face: eyes meeting eyes. *That* child was willing to smile at her; that child would *always* smile at her. That child would never find fault with her. That child would never punish her or speak coldly to her or turn away in impatience and irritation, leaving her crying unconsoled. That child would always have time to play. That child would always care for her, always give her approval. That child would be sad when she was sad, and that would take the sadness away. Even if no one else could be trusted, the child could trust *that* child, for she could be summoned at will. The child, in her bleak helplessness, finally had something she could count on completely. If the world looked scary or uninviting or undependable, she could find this place with that child and be safe. And she, the living child, could be there for that child as well; she could tend her and feed her and help her grow strong and healthy. Together, they could be perfect and beautiful and everyone would love them and take care of them, the way they really deserved.

He watched as the pair of them, flesh and image, danced with each other in a symmetry and perfection that no two living beings could ever manage. Even in company, they would always be able to steal glances at each other across the room, checking in for a sweet dose of approbation. In times of conflict, they could take refuge in each other's unblinking kindness, hiding untouched until the storm passed. And safe in each other's unconditional positive regard, they could put firmly away from themselves that underlying sense—the really scary monster-under-the-bed one—that some-how, something was horribly wrong with them. *I must have done something wrong, I don't know what, but there must have been something I did, or maybe it's who I am, and that's why They don't love me. I must have been bad. I can't be bad again, not ever.* So badness was out. If, by any chance, something bad did happen, they could not possibly have done it, because they were such good children and good children *never* do bad things.

The child made him feel so wrenched with pity and kindness and deep love that tears stung his eyes. He wanted to pick her up, wipe her face clean, change her wet clothing, feed her warm bread and fresh milk. He longed to hold her in the crook of his arm, stroking her hair and letting her rest her head on his shoulder, where she could cry as she needed to cry and be helpless and trust-ing again. He wanted to tell her over and over, until the truth sank in and soothed the terrible hurt in her: *No, it wasn't your fault that They couldn't love you. Maybe it wasn't their fault either. But you deserve to be truly loved.*

He knew, though, that the child he'd be cradling, even if he could reach and lift her, was more than half glass by now. You can't stay a child looking in the mirror for love, or not for very long, or you become only your own image, with not much of the real child still inside, and that not able to grow the way a soul should grow. The child's only reality had become the mirror and its safety, and there she stayed frozen. Sometimes, in years to come, she'd have a dim uneasy sense that maybe it wasn't supposed to be this way, but then she would turn away from the bad thought and back to her friend for reassurance, and they would chant in unison: *We're fine just the way we are, it's true, it's really true.*

He remembered finding a robin's egg last summer: the egg was uncracked and still egg-heavy, but clearly the embryo in it must have died unhatched, very sad. He didn't know whether or not a soul could die, but he was pretty sure that it could get stuck in one spot, either for lack of nourishment or from deep wounding, maybe both. This child would never get any bigger, not really, not as long as she depended on that child in the mirror. The ache of love and pity stayed with him, but he knew that he had nothing to offer that could do her any good. Only God can heal damage that happens so early and goes so deep.

He felt such sorrow for her. He knew that anyone who loved her or saw her with any clear kindness would feel this same sorrow—but not she herself. As long as the mirror was her safe and happy place, as long as she and that child fed and loved and played with each other and none other, she'd have only a mirror's depth, no more; and sorrow, like love and real self-knowledge, goes much too deep for mirrors. She would always refuse to rub up against the warm, coarse, maddening roughness of this world; the only surface she could tolerate was smooth and cool and frictionless and perfect, and about three-sixteenths of an inch deep. So she would never have real sorrow. And that, he thought, was the worst sorrow of all.

The child's image shrank to a pinpoint and vanished, and with it his sorrowing love. He shook his head, clearing the last wisps away, feeling suddenly full of light and energy. *God, when was the last time I felt like this?* He found that he was sitting on the side porch steps being lightly rained on. The rain felt wonderful, light and cool and delicious as a Bach flute sonata, and he held his hands out in delight, singing with abandoned tunelessness, reaching for the drops happily, greedily. He stayed there until the rain stopped. And then he went indoors and upstairs, and he changed into dry clothes, and he started to pack.

# STILL LIFE, WITH DRAGONS

It had been raining for weeks, or so it seemed. The damp was so thick and constant it got into her dreams. She dreamed, for example, that things started to grow in her apartment: young trees sprouting from the hot-air registers in the hallway, vines snaking around the edges of the bedroom ceiling, mushrooms in her clean white kitchen, sprouting from the draining board.

And in her dreams, he stood at the bedroom window in the rain, pale-faced and sweet as apples, begging to be let in. He'd always known just how to moderate his charm: too much, and she might clue in, be put on guard. A light touch, he'd learned, worked best. So in her dreams, he still had that old mild self-deprecating childlike sweetness that she'd never been able to say no to. It was pasted all over his face, in her dream, and she closed the curtains, leaving him out in the wet.

Strangely, she never flinched or worried when someone knocked on her door: she knew, rationally, that he was with another woman out on the coast, having found someone (as he'd found her, years past) who would "finally love" him—that is, who would put him first, last, and always. Since she herself was not the first person to "finally love" him, she was by no means surprised to learn that another woman would be just as big a fool. We all want to be needed; it makes us feel valued, important. Truism. Hardly anyone's clever enough to see through it while it's actually happening. She had acquired a certain rueful self-knowledge that she fully intended to hang on to with both hands for the rest of her life.

He would not actually come back, or call, or try to make any contact with her at all: she knew that. In the end he'd disgraced himself completely, and he knew it, and she knew it too, and he could not possibly live with that. The neighbors, fed up and frightened by the noise, had called the police, and the police saw the situation with a simple hard clarity that totally ignored his convoluted reasoning and the dark romanticism in which he wrapped his own behavior. She had not pressed charges, but that was the end of it. With those two quiet, bulky blue-uniformed presences in the living room taking notes, she'd finally *seen* him, seen him accurately, unbent by love or pity, and that was the thing he could not stand. They both reached the same unspoken agreement, that this end was final. She knew, in that sense, that she had nothing to worry about. Knew it in her head, at any rate.

So why in her dreams did he move back in, bringing this rampant swamplike greenery with him? Why did she dream about his seeping under the front door like a shadow or a bad smell, dripping from the ceiling like a leak, softening the plaster until it came crashing down on her? Why did it haunt her, that he was ill and dying and that it was her job to nurse him?

And where did these weird sudden sharp flakes of memory come from? If asked, of course she would expect to have memories of him; they had, after all, lived together for almost ten years, more than enough time to lay down a whole ocean floor of memory. But in fact she remembered relatively little: whole months had apparently gone completely unrecorded, so that she had to grapple on to landmarks ("I got that promotion in '92") and reason backward and forward in time to place a particular event. And the memories she had from her time with him were completely different from the memories she had of normal times—why did that phrase drift into her head, "normal times"? They were abrupt, vivid, unrelated, like chips of obsidian; they had no context and no color. She could remember what happened—his face transformed, his voice thickened, rising from comfortable bass to screaming tenor, her arms up in front of her face, herself curled on the kitchen floor—but not what she'd felt or thought. Nothing. These pictures would come unsummoned to her while she stared out the bus window on the way to work or stood by the xerox machine or bought pork chops for supper on the way home. They would arrive, flying in from

God knows where, while she sorted laundry or reorganized the fridge: frozen, sharp flakes that should have stung, should have pierced her hide and left her bleeding. But she felt nothing. Only, sometimes, she had the oddest longing to slash her own hide, even go for her eyes. These impulses never frightened her; they came and went quite calmly, almost comforting.

The dreams (now that she thought about them) were similarly bland and unaffecting. She never felt frightened, even as the vines reached down from the ceiling and started crawling across her dresser top and down into the drawer where his socks had been, where she now kept her scarves. She felt only mild exasperation: *Goddammit! Where did I put the clippers?* As (in her dream) a young larch, gray-stemmed, strong and lithe as a cat, pushed up from the cold-air return vent in the living room, growing another fifteen inches as she watched it, she felt the way she felt whenever the cat threw up on the carpet; she wanted to whisk herself out of the room, snapping the door shut behind her. *I'll come back and deal with this later.* But she had no sense of the monstrosity of it all, no sense that it was in any way gothic or even odd to have a jungle taking over an ordinary ground-floor flat in a nice old building in a city neighborhood. It felt, in fact, quite commonplace.

She got up—it was absurdly early, but she had no wish to go back to sleep—put on her dressing gown, and went to make herself a cup of tea, trying to shake herself out of this strange state. As she waited for the kettle to boil, she had a sudden disturbing image of her mind as a mirror, a round mirror maybe a foot across: the glass itself was clear and clean and quite straightforward, but it was surrounded by a frame of strange and baroque shells and other things that she couldn't quite identify. She felt fine as long as she looked in the mirror, seeing her own quite unremarkable face with its normal straight fine hair, neatly cut; but in her side vision, the frame seemed to squirm. She didn't want to see it. It might be something she'd have to deal with.

*It might be something she'd have to deal with.*

He had been (she now realized) like a man with a dragon looking over his shoulder; he was studiously avoiding looking at the dragon, and she (trying to accept his point of view and see things from where he stood) had pretended too that no dragon was there, until she genuinely stopped seeing it—in fact, saw no dragon-shaped space, nothing whatsoever even faintly dragony. But the cops had looked at the animal most clearly and dispassionately; and while they hadn't named it, hadn't typed the specimen and entered it into any taxonomy, they had made it clear that some sort of fire-breathing beast was in the room. And standing where they were standing, and looking at him from their point of view, she saw it for the first time clearly: both how small and sad the dragon was, and how small and sad he was in his desperate attempt to pretend it wasn't there. After that, things could never be the same between them. They both knew that, without having to speak it.

But it was funny, how bloodless her present pity for him felt; how calmly she could regard the desperate weakness that they'd both worked so hard to ignore. She felt compassion for him, but it was compassion with the living pith removed—bone with the marrow scooped out. She could understand now his old reproach:

that she didn't love him, had no feeling for him, didn't really care. She could see her own remoteness. *Maybe I'm just a cold person,* she thought. *But I wasn't always.*

Standing with the tea bag in her hand, as the kettle screamed ignored, she wondered: *When was the last time I felt anything? I don't remember.* She could remember times in the past when she had, in fact, been full of feeling: moments of acute joy or the pain that makes you walk into walls. But even those memories were glazed over; she could stand with her fingertips on a cool clear surface, looking through at her younger self in laughter or tears, but without any real recognition. So much stood between her and that younger self that these memories were words with the music stripped out.

She poured water into a mug, dropped in the tea bag and stirred. She realized, wondering, that even these recognitions had no real color to them, no emotional force. She felt a vague sadness about this state of affairs, disquiet and a certain gentle loss. A friend of hers on Prozac talked about something similar; he'd lost his crushing depression, but he reported a strange flatness and a wistful sense that something was going on that he couldn't be part of: a party that he felt excluded from, a range of colors he could no longer see.

She pulled out the bag, squeezed it dry, and reached for her compost bucket—a small covered plastic container she kept under the sink for vegetable peelings and other compostable stuff. Every week or two, she emptied it onto the compost bin that some green-minded tenants had set up behind the apartment building.

She thought vaguely that it was probably about time to take the stuff out again, as she pulled the bucket out and popped off the sealed lid.

And almost threw up or screamed when a cloud of fruit flies burst upward, drifting into her crisp, white, immaculate kitchen.

She slammed the bucket lid back on and grabbed a tea towel, flapping it wildly, slamming a half dozen flies up against the refrigerator door. They were expanding into the kitchen air like a miasma, like a toxic spill, uncontrollable. She heard someone yelling curses and wondered what the neighbors would think, and then she realized that it was she herself and that now she was pounding on the refrigerator with both fists while feral noises came unbidden from her throat. She spun around the kitchen, a jerky ballerina, electrified by rage, whipped by it as by lightning, bouncing off the counters, making bruises she would not know about until later, as she slapped at the flies and at her own face with all the strength she had, and howled.

Her tea mug—her favorite—lay in shards on the floor, and there were tea stains on the white curtains and blood on the floor where she'd cut her foot on one of the bits of china. She herself was hanging on to the sink edge gasping, her hair hanging into her eyes as the tears washed down her cheeks and her nose spilled snot onto the porcelain. She grabbed a paper towel and mopped at her face, and her fingers wouldn't hold the towel or support her anymore, so she slid down to the floor, curling once again into fetal position, knees drawn up, waiting for his foot.

Much later—too late to pull herself together for work, going by the sun's angle—she crawled into the bathtub, which she had filled almost to overflowing with the hottest water she could find. Wincing, she slid into it and reached for the shampoo. She washed her hair five times, unable to stop. She found she was crooning comfort to herself, singing herself a lullaby, hugging herself, stroking her own arms and shoulders, murmuring loving concern and gently touching her bruises like a mother holding on her lap a child with a skinned knee.

It was a beginning. The joy of it leapt in her, even as another wave of pain slapped her and spun her around and water sploshed over the tub side onto the floor. She turned on the hot tap and held her finger under the scalding water, just for a second, not long enough to harm herself, but *feeling* it, glorying in sensation. *I am alive.* And: *Where does it go from here?*

A burst of energy lifted her out of the water, decisively. She toweled herself off, looking into the steamy mirror and considering the great green-gold form, splendidly baroque, whose ruby eyes met her gray ones in the glass, who added its steam to the bath steam: *Oh yes, you are my own, my very own, my dragon.* She wished she could turn and put her arm around its scaly neck. *Shall we try very hard, dear one, not to fry anything we shouldn't?*

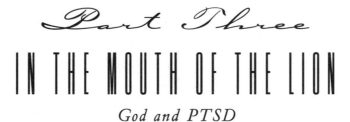

# Part Three

# IN THE MOUTH OF THE LION

*God and PTSD*

# SCENE FROM A MALL

I am ascending slowly on a long escalator in a large
shopping center in the city. I came in on the ground floor, and the
shop I want is on the third floor, so I'm spending quite a while
standing here as the metal step beneath me slides steadily upward.
Actually, it's more than that: we seem to have entered one of those
odd little warps where time slows down to a moderate crawl,
stretching or sagging like a clothesline with too many wet towels
on it. These things happen. I don't know why; black holes or
something.

Gently rising like a god in a box, I look down at the people
below me as they mill through the warm open glossy mall space

(what do you call a hallway in a mall, anyway?). They are the standard mixture: girls, kewl or giggly, showing off their slenderness and youth and brand-new perfection; boys, definitely kewl (or trying to be, anyway), slouching along, carefully not gawking at the girls; matrons, neat but not gaudy, made up a little too thickly and with hair just the slightest bit too rigid; bureaucrats in their obligatory winter attire (fur hat with fold-down earflaps, dark long coat with astrakhan collar, high rubber galoshes); sleek young businessthingies more dashingly dressed, tilting their polished heads against their cell phones; fresh young couples with their first baby in the new, beautiful stroller . . . oh, you know the lot, unless you live in some out-of-the-way spot like the Magdalen Islands or the Northeast Kingdom of Vermont, where they know better.

It all looks so normal—and then the world does one of its tiny shifts, so small I can't even feel the escalator step shimmy under my feet; and I am looking down at people who are completely alien from me. They are so foreign they might as well be from Tierra del Fuego. They feel so weirdly *other* to me that they might as well be Martians or even Betelgeusians. Their closed, blank, well-groomed faces sit in front of heads that I can't even guess the contents of. I cannot imagine what they think. I cannot imagine how they experience life. And I know that they cannot imagine how I experience life.

I am rural; they are urban. They are almost all well dressed and buffed to the max; I am scruffy and slightly untidy, sneaker laces always coming adrift, face tired and too expressive, hair up to God knows what, in my cheap baggy cotton trousers and jacket that needs cleaning. They are moving with apparent purpose and intention, comfortable in this setting, while I drift, always at severe risk for getting lost, slightly overcome by all the stores and the sheer number of warm bodies.

I make eye contact. They don't. They are well. I am not. Not now, at least.

That last, of all things, is the Plexiglas wall between us: they can't know where I am or where I've come from. If I spoke of my experience, would they turn away? Probably; most people don't know much about handling difficult subjects, and my past is difficult. I try not to let it run my life, but it's *there,* like a big stone tortoise in the middle of the parlor carpet: you can get used to it, see it as an ordinary part of life, but you can't pretend it's not there. Could I explain what this disorder is, why I need space around me and can't manage being bumped or crowded? Someone drops a parcel, bang!—and I do my startle reaction and get a couple of sideways looks from people who clearly (or so I think!) wonder what's wrong with me. Could I explain? No. We're Canadians, remember.

They don't get it—why should they?—and I'm not about to enlighten them. That's out: we don't bare our infirmities in public, because that would startle the horses. We are careful not to impose on strangers here. These mall people are healthy and normal. I am many things, but right now, and for most of the past and the foreseeable future, normal isn't one of them. And in my imagination, the clear hard distance between us thickens by another inch or three.

It's easy, in this strung-out pocket of time, to turn my suddenly strong sense of alienation over in my hand like a freshly precious pebble, admiring it from all angles, tasting its complexities, lovingly discovering its nuances, carefully mapping each tiny indentation, each shading. Isn't that what the romantics did, after all?—and while I think the fashion may be getting a tad passé, there are still romantics around, lots of them, speaking of alienation as though it were the only possible state of mind for an intelligent, sensitive person, and anyone who's unalienated must be totally brain-dead, a real Pollyanna, or in deep denial—DUH!

I could get off the escalator at the top, and lean over the upper-floor railing, gazing down at these people, despising them as ordinary petit bourgeois, unenlightened, inexperienced in the true shittiness of life—utterly unselfaware, totally naive. Or I could take the other road of contempt: *Well, \*you\* may be sleek and prosperous and unscrewed-up, but \*\*\*I\*\*\* am an Artist, and a Spiritually Enlightened Artist to boot, and I betcha you don't even know what "eschatology" means, much less how to spell it.* Or maybe I could fuse the two approaches. Yeah. I could do that and still claim to be a Christian. I don't think so.

I do know Envy when it bites me, after all, and both this sense of alienation and the underlying anger are really envy—envy that these people have probably had it comparatively easy and I didn't, envy that they seem to have it all together and are happy while I'm still floundering after all these years. But Envy, however natural, is still one of the Seven Deadlies. It is, above all, a non-grown-up emotion, and I have faint hopes of becoming an adult one of these years. If that's what I want, then Envy's one thing I have to put behind me, like ever being size 12 again. And that means putting aside alienation as well.

So how does a person do that? By figuring out what the problem is and turning it inside out. What do I want from these people, really—what would I ask for, if I could? I think I'd ask for them to understand me and accept me, just as I am, ugly teeth and PTSD and all. Isn't that what most of us dream of—to be seen and seen as lovable? I'd like to turn on this escalator step and say in a voice that had some chance of reaching them: *People, please don't judge me by how I look. Let me tell you a bit about my story.*

But how can I think of wanting these perfect strangers to understand and accept me when I'm so eager to judge and reject them, unknown and untalked to? How can I ask them to care about me first, when I don't care for them? How can I mourn because I think they could never understand my experience or what it has done to me, when I don't have two consecutive clues what their experience is? Maybe they have griefs and joys that I can't possibly understand either. Who among these people has cancer, or an adulterous spouse, or a pink slip in pocket or purse? Who's still being abused, and who is still recovering from abuse? Who has anxiety attacks apparently for no good reason? Who is struggling with grief or schizophrenia? Who's facing bankruptcy? Which of them really is happy and balanced and quite all right? I have no way of knowing, not from watching them scuttle through this mall.

These people are *people*—not ants crawling over that polished white marble floor, undistinguishable one from the next, but *souls,* each as beloved by God as Mother Teresa. Some of them are probably pretty badly behaved or selfish or cruel, and others of them are probably really good people, and most are in the middle, just like me. What do I have in common with them? Humanity, for starters: instincts and dreams, knowing the ins and outs of a Canadian winter, loving some people, hating others, experiencing disappointments, being afraid, feeling lonely, giving and taking injustice, lying awake in the small hours worrying about money. We have more in common than we have apart.

It's so easy to mock those bureaucrats, for instance. This is a civil-service city, and find me one of those without all sorts of civil-servant jokes, funny because they're so pointed. But they must hurt. I think of one of the most bureaucratic-looking civil servants I know, a mild-mannered man just past fifty, apparently a fusspot with the right sort of galoshes, and I think how different he is from how he seems—how full of sharpness and wit and deep kindness he is, how his spirit quests and leaps playfully as he boards his unremarkable bus for the quiet ride home to suburbia. I resolve to remember in future to thank God every day because my work doesn't bore me into paralysis and I don't have to cope with office politics.

Those young girls in their early beauty: I can remember sixteen, and it was no fun whatsoever. Maybe it's time I thought about unclenching my memory-fist from that sense of failure, because I wasn't bonelessly slender, or pretty and well dressed, or popular. Maybe, instead of envying their lissome waists and perfect tiny butts, I should remember what it was like to be a teenaged girl, and how little I want to go back there. I remember the Uglies. Show me a teenaged girl without the Uglies, and I'll show you someone who's been knocked unconscious. Thank you; I'll live with this body, so long as I can have all the other things that come with middle age.

Those boys: I have sons that age, and I know all about the public mask that has so little to do with the hopeful, vulnerable, scared, and lonely kid behind it. Being a teenaged boy is no picnic. I hope their parents love them, that's what; I hope their parents actually *listen*, because by building up your patience when your son narrates a computer game until you want to scream, you tell the kid that Mother or Dad is actually willing to give you a real hearing, and that makes it okay to talk about some things you might otherwise feel you have to keep to yourself. I hope they have people to talk to, these boys. I hope they have some place of safety, somewhere to loosen up and be human and giddy.

Those highly surfaced matrons: probably each and every one is trying to juggle family and job and maybe aging parents as well; each one frets continually that she's not getting it right. How many of them go to bed most nights so exhausted and strung out with things left undone that they can't get to sleep, or wake far too early with a "to do" list unscrolling behind their sandy heavy eyelids? Ladies, been there, done that; shove over and make room on the bench and let's hoist a well-deserved glass of wine, shall we?

These people can't reach through this Plexiglas wall to touch and love and care for me. They don't know that that's what I'm secretly wanting, and even if they did, how many of us can do that, really?—recognize a stranger's unspoken need and grab the courage to do something about it? Jesus could do that. I'm not Jesus. Why should I expect them to do for me far more than I could do for them?

Maybe these people secretly want the same understanding and love, and yet are incapable of understanding and acknowledging that desire to themselves or anyone else. They may feel the emptiness that signals a lonely ache in the God-shaped hole. They may feel as profoundly alienated from each other and me as I felt, a moment ago, from them. Who knows?

With a flick of my mind, I restart time, and the ridged steel step slides gracefully flat at the top of the escalator, and I do my little klutzy "which foot do I use to get off an escalator?" shuffle, the Mark of the Rube. I stop by the railing and lean on it looking down, trying to see these people as God sees them. I can't do it, of course. God knows their lives as God knows mine—which is to say, better than they or I know our own lives. God alone knows how our experiences arrive, or what they make of us, or what we make of them. But God does the loving *first*. He doesn't wait to be loved and understood, and if he did wait, he'd have to wait forever, because which of us is capable of seeing God well enough to love him as he deserves?

So maybe that's the pattern I should try to follow. I can't expect people to accept me all unknown, reaching through the Plexiglas to give me what I can't even acknowledge I need. I have to try to love them first, to *see* them, to try to find out what we have to share, not what keeps us apart. I have to do this not in any expectation of being loved back, because earned love is a slight and unreliable thing, but because that's what the currency of human exchange really ought to be about.

If all I have to offer others is resentment, bitterness, self-centeredness, and a sense of my own damaged separateness, then I have no right to complain (or feel superior!) about feeling alienated, because it's my own doing, not the world's. I can't judge them with neither justice nor mercy and yet expect them to accept me as I am. I can't ask for their acceptance if I'm not ready to accept them. All I can do is offer whatever I have to give: a thought of kindness, the imagination of love.

You gets what you gives. That's the truth.

> *I can't bring you love if you don't love;*
> *And I can't bring you time if you ain't got time;*
> *And I can't bring you strength, baby, if you ain't strong;*
> *And I can't bring you kindness if you ain't kind;*
> *I can't bring you kindness if you ain't kind.* *

*Mary Chapin Carpenter, "It Don't Bring You," *State of the Heart* (Columbia Records, 1989).

# ABSOLUTELY ELSEWHERE

It's a strange sensation, not exactly unpleasant—since when is numbness and distance unpleasant?—but maybe a little unsettling. I think I could probably invoke it at will, if I tried, but I don't. I get here often enough, thank you.

It's a state of mild distance from things. If the things being said to me were horrible and hurtful—and I've had vitriolic hatred heaved in my direction often and often, words I still can't really remember because my memory refused to store them—then I could put up this shield of remoteness, and the poison would roll right off it like raindrops off plastic. Or so I thought, anyway. Turns out that another part of my brain sucked up the poison like a sponge and stored it separately, apart from my memory proper; so that the memory itself is colorless, only mildly and academically interesting, while the strong emotions, colors that would sear your eyeballs, are memoryless, adrift, apparently coming out of nowhere.

Yes, I know that sounds wonky. It *is* wonky. But it's how you survive, at the time. The mind, like the body, has its own ways of going into shock in order to protect its own vitality from mortal hurt. If you can't live with whatever it is, war or abuse or what have you, and you have to live with it (or feel you must), then you develop ways of trying to shed the hurt instead of letting it drive you down.

But then it gets easier and easier to zone out. Suddenly you're above and outside life itself, like a soul bereft of body bobbing hazily near the ceiling and looking down. Or you find reality it-self abruptly constricting into a sort of tunnel, the sides of which are insubstantial, nothing more than bent and blurry light—but the light-wall's too real to break through, and it parts you from the life buzzing around you, that frightens you so much. One way or an-other, you've dissociated. There's you over here and reality over there, and you've become disconnected, because it's so much easier that way.

It's easier too to turn away from much of life, because, dammit, life *hurts*. For all you've built up such beautiful defenses of re-moteness and zoning out, whenever you get into real contact with anyone, you always seem to get bruised in particularly painful ways. One problem with this disorder is that it leaves you acting like a lobster: hard shell out, trembling vulnerability locked away. Coming out of the shell is just cruisin' for a bruisin'; you've learned that over and over again. The only really safe place is off here in this strange involuntary numbness, away from the risks, set aside in your remoteness. So you limit your contacts with the people who don't understand how you got here, whose misjudgment hurts, but whom you can't begin to talk to because you're not speaking the same language—you aren't even on the same planet, really. But that makes life so lonely, so terribly lonely—and then, there you are, nipped in the pliers: fear of hurt squeezing one side of you, loneliness squeezing the other side. Not good.

Besides, you can't imagine anyone wanting to keep you company, such a lump of no-good misery as you are sometimes. Maybe you have memories that so shame you that all you want to do is curl into a ball, like an armadillo, and die, just die, because when you die, so will the memories. Or maybe someone convinced you that you'd deserved what happened: *I didn't do anything wrong, and besides, you made me do it:* that was the statement you were supposed to swallow without for a moment seeing how sheerly nutzoid it is. Funny, how easily you swallowed it, accepting it into your innermost being. For at one level, we all still think as we did in kindergarten, with a child's crystalline impeccably wrong reasoning: Bad Things Happen to Bad People, and Good Things Happen to Good People. Bad Things Have Happened to Me, and since Bad Things Don't Happen to Good People, what's the inescapable conclusion? For you "know" that if you were good enough and strong enough, you wouldn't be like this. You wouldn't be broken.

This is all swirling around your head like a dust storm in a dreary landscape: alienation, numbness, loneliness, self-blame, all so mixed up that you can't tell where the one ends and the next be-gins. It's deeply preoccupying. And for that reason, you are not aware of the quiet presence hunkered down beside you. This was someone who kept you company through all the horrors, whatever they were. This is someone who suffered it all with you—has suf-fered much more than you can possibly imagine, and all because all he wants is for you to let him be close to you.

But you're so fixed on your loneliness that you can't feel him near you. You don't trust him to *be*, not really; he could so easily be a figment of your hopeful imagination. And even if the sensa-tion of him comes back over and over again, until you're not sure if you're dreaming him or if he's really there—even then, you're not at all sure you want this intrusion into your solitude. It's your private place, after all, your one infinitely precious safety zone, the one place you can't be hurt, even if it's lonely sometimes. But it's only safe because you own it, you control it, nobody else is allowed in: "I'll go into my mind and close the door / And you won't bother me anymore."

And how could you possibly trust him, when he didn't help when you needed help so very badly? You don't think you might be angry at him; you can't be angry at such perfect indifference, any more than you could be angry at a boulder that just squatted there by the side of the road as two cars on black ice slid into each other in terrible slow motion. If you think about him at all (and you try not to, not really) you might think of him as the Unmoved Mover, who started it all and now sits back, perfect and cold as marble, as the suffering universe unfolds around him. That's the only version of him you can stand to think about, because all the alternatives are horrible.

Still, there he sits, a quiet presence, companionable, not speaking, but in a silence that feels close as your skin.

*Lord, you have searched me out and known me;*
*you know when I sit down and when I rise up;*
*you discern my thoughts from far away.*
*You search out my path and my lying down,*
*and are acquainted with all my ways.*

Not only that, but he has been with you all along, even when you weren't capable of feeling his companionship:

*Where can I go from your spirit?*
*Or where can I flee from your presence?*
*If I ascend to heaven, you are there.*
*If I make my bed in hell, you are there. . . .*
*If I say, "Surely the darkness shall cover me,*
*and the light around me become night,"*
*even the darkness is not dark to you;*
*the night is as bright as the day,*
*for darkness is as light to you.*

He was there with you in the darkness that you don't want to remember, because when you remember it, you go back there, and you don't want to see that place ever again. He was with you, and he suffered everything that you suffered, as he has always been willing to keep us company in the dark times. When you slip into the darkness again, when the memories come back, and the nightmares, and the sudden flashes of disconcerting déjà vu—then he reaches out, saying in the gentlest tone right under your mind's surface: *You aren't alone. I'm here. I will stay with you, whatever.* The voice is quiet, unintrusive: almost more an infinitely peaceful space into which the words flow, fresh and soft as water: *Child, I love you. I love you, child, my child.*

Now I know to listen to that voice and to trust that it is real and dependable. Now I find sometimes that when I'm in that odd state of dissociation, I can sense that God's in here with me. And then it's not so much loneliness as a quiet time between friends. It's not quite the same thing as zoning out or becoming numb, this sense of quietness; it's more meditative. It's still a rest from the pain and the turmoil, but it's no longer the unnatural quiet of frozenness. It's a healthy sort of rest, a place where I can be private with the one whose love always did sustain me, even when I didn't know it was there.

Maybe I'll always zone out when life seems to be more than I can cope with, or when something jars my memories loose. But maybe when I find myself in that strange tunnel, with a nightmare a couple of turns behind me but still within smelling range—maybe then I'll be able to turn again and again to the quietness that walks with me. And I will say, "You still here, God?" And he will say, "Yes. Always was. Always will be."

# DANCING HICCUPS

On the wall of the downstairs bathroom of the house where I grew up, there was a cartoon that I still remember in vivid detail and with much appreciation. The cartoon showed a street corner, with sidewalk and street sign. Hanging on to the street-sign pole and leaning away from it was a woman, wearing a hat. Only a hat, nothing else. Her hair was wild, her expression was demented, and she was grinning like a fiend. The caption: "Public opinion no longer worries me."

I was remembering this the other day, when somebody slammed a door upstairs and I just about jumped out of my skin. Perhaps the most characteristic symptom of this stupid disorder is what they call the startle reflex—an exaggerated response to sudden bangs and rattles. When I'm at my worst, all it takes is the phone ringing and I have to be peeled off the ceiling. A truck backfires in the street and I'm two feet off the ground, thrashing wildly and yipping quite audibly.

All I can say, if I'm stuck with this, is that it's a damn good thing I don't have any dignity left . . . But then I had to reconsider that thought, because it's only half true. There's dignity and dignity, after all. There's skin-dignity: our presentation (usually more our pretense!) of poise, composure, decorum, self-possession. Skin-dignity is how we show the world that we've everything well under control, that we're cool in a crisis, that we're unscarred and unblemished and just fine right down to our insteps—that we've got it all together, thank you very much.

But then there's soul-dignity: the sense that we're children of God, beloved just as we are and therefore capable of being not all right without losing that sense of being loved and lovable. Soul-dignity knows something about respecting others and expecting proper respect, because it understands the worth of everyone's soul, your own included. Soul-dignity is patient and enduring in the face of oppression. Soul-dignity finds resources in the strangest, darkest, wildest places, and keeps on keeping on.

Skin-dignity can't afford to twitch and yip. Soul-dignity knows how little twitching and yipping matter.

I can think of quite a number of people I know and love who have a whole lot of soul-dignity and not much skin-dignity: one friend with Tourette's syndrome, another with anxiety disorder that's thrown his digestive system into spasms, another with multiple sclerosis, another with depressions that leave her paralyzed for weeks, sometimes months. What about my mother's friend with throat cancer? What about the boy-child, now over twenty, who has cerebral palsy and irreversible brain damage from his botched birth and who will always be in diapers, cooing unintelligibly to the air around him and laughing at his own inner marvels? For each and every one of these, skin-dignity isn't on; their infirmities are right out there, undisguisable, for the whole world to witness. But each has a hard-won soul-dignity—except for the boy, whose soul-dignity is the purest of God-gifts. And that soul-dignity is a thing of beauty and a joy forever.

And then I think of the people I know who rank skin-dignity very high indeed: teenagers, for example, who are so terribly concerned with appearances and what people will think. But most of them, thank God, outgrow skin-dignity after life shakes them up and down and gooses them once or twice. The people I know who have gotten stuck on saving their skin-dignity at all costs usually paid prices that I don't really want to think about: careers and marriages mostly. If you can't stand being seen with your love handles and the bags under your eyes and the occasional uncontrollable hiccup, you're not going to be able to maintain loving intimacy at all well, over time. It's as though the skin-dignity puppet stands in for the soul-dignity person, the one growing as the other seems to diminish. Now that I think of it, maybe it's a two-way street: that is, skin-dignity and soul-dignity are inversely related. One goes up, the other goes down.

I'm not holding out for humiliation as a Positive Uplifting Experience. It isn't. And probably it's even more negative for the humiliator as for the humiliatee; you can maintain some sense of soul-dignity even in the face of humiliation, whereas the person inflicting the humiliation suffers real soul-dignity damage. How can people think of themselves as good and worthy of love when they've behaved that badly? They have no choice but to block the memory out, or set it somewhere where they don't really have to look at it, and to invest more and more in skin-dignity—whether it's charm or a handsome uniform—to preserve some sense of self-worth. Or maybe they figure that if they reduce their victims to the breaking point, they'll be on the same level once again. "See? You're really no better than I am."

But if you can manage to hang on to some portion of your soul even under horripilating circumstances—if you can manage a little love, the odd small soul-making act of generosity or grace—then your own soul-dignity grows, even as your skin-dignity is stripped from you a piece at a time. If you're broken, and you can accept being broken and make whatever peace you can with God and yourself, then you have negated the breaking, and you've added a chunk of weight to your soul-dignity. And then skin-dignity looks as silly as it really is.

I knew an old woman, years and years ago—I suspect she's dead now, and happy in God's hands—who had survived internment in a Japanese prisoner-of-war camp in Indonesia. She had gone into the camp with a husband and child, and she had come out alone. I used to see her on the bus, her worn hands folded serenely in her lap, her white hair looking like something had roosted in it, and her faded blue eyes full of a deep peace. I'm sure that the nightmares came back often—the terrors in the night and the waking strangeness, in which you walk in quite another time with Pain and Fear at your right and left hands. I'm sure that she too startled easily. I think she might have been just a little crazy. But oh, her soul had such a weight of dignity that indeed "public opinion no longer worried her."

When David brought the Ark of the Covenant up to Jerusalem, he and all the house of Israel danced before it with all their might. They danced like fools, and they sang and shouted and carried on as though they were crazy or pissed to the gills— just as later, at Pentecost, the Spirit-filled disciples carried on in a babel of different languages and got accused of being drunk. David danced before God without the least thought of kingly propriety, wearing only a linen cloth. His wife, Michal—Saul's daughter, who had loved David so much—looked down from her window and despised him: how could the King of Israel behave like a vulgar fellow, exposing himself to the lowest of the low? But David knew: we are to be fools to God, trusting him so much that our skin-dignity doesn't matter a pinch of cold mashed potatoes, because God values your soul and mine so very, very much.

God does not choose us because we dress in power suits and carry leather briefcases and have perfectly turned-out shoes. God chooses us because he loves us in our sneakers and with our twitches and hiccups. God loves us when we fall over for no particularly good reason, or say something really stupid, or we laugh far too loud, especially in church. God strengthens the soul's dignity, if we're willing to stop clutching the rags of our skin-dignity—as though those rags weren't perfectly transparent anyway. . . .

"God chose what is foolish in the world to shame the wise; God chose what is weak in the world to shame the strong." Therefore we can afford to be foolish; we can afford to be weak. "For God's foolishness is greater than man's wisdom; and God's weakness is greater than human strength."

And public opinion no longer worries me.

# SNOW PILE

Some days are better than others, and this one was an "other"—a day for startlements and hypersensitivity and a sense of being in a long tunnel along with a nightmare. The nightmare isn't close, but it's still within smelling range.

So it was a mistake to go to the supermarket. I needed things—pancake mix, beef for supper, more milk (always more milk!). But it was a busy Saturday afternoon and the aisles were full of people, each in his or her own particular maze of being, none really aware of all the other people around. I got bumped into once or twice, jumping out of my skin and flinching back, banged carts with another woman—nothing out of the ordinary,

but much more than I could handle. And then too, properly considered, a supermarket is a stunningly rich field of stimuli: colors,
shapes, people, odors, sounds, all normally full of lively interest,
but not when all your senses are bare naked, tender to the light-
est breeze, and shivering in the world's noisiness. I got through
it all somehow, huddling in the quieter aisles, biding my time until it was safe to whiz through the vegetable section. I probably
looked nuts. I don't care.

Got home, only to realize that I hadn't mailed the insurance
premium payments, so instead of taking the car out again, I decided to walk downtown to the post office. I figured the walk
might calm me, soothe the jangling down. It's a beautiful late-
March day, a little chilly but brilliantly sunny. I bundled up in winter coat, big scarf and gloves, and started down the street through
the beauty of the day . . .

. . . only to find that that wasn't really a good idea either. Mild
as the cold was, it ached like January bitterness on my forehead,
stung my cheeks like a slap, and nipped the inside of my nose. The
sky was a lovely deep blue and the sun was warm on my face—
but the light, mild to anyone in his right mind but not to me in
my not-right mind, made my eyeballs feel fried. I had to squint
against it, and that narrowed my view down to a slit. It wasn't
cheering; it was overwhelming. No comfort there, out walking
through my town, where at least a little comfort almost always is.
Damn.

If there's one piece of Christian discipline I've learned, it's that
you can usually redeem something, however bad it is, by making

a conscious effort to point it Godward. The Something may or may not get any easier to live with, but at least it gets more in-teresting. If you're doing suffering for the moment, one of the sor-rier side effects is that once you're past the initial "ping!" reactions, suffering becomes *boring*. It takes all the interest out of life. Turning whatever-it-is in God's direction at least gives you some-thing to think about, other than the suffering-thing itself.

So I prayed for God to take this @#$%#@ hypersensitivity and make something of it, before it drove me nuts. And on the way back from the post office, there it was, a gift, a bone for my senses to chew on: the snow.

Cold as it's been, the sun's been bright enough and the air mild enough that most of the snow we had has melted into the street or ground or into the air itself by sublimation, the same way moth-balls dissolve without melting. We are in late March. It's been known to snow in April around here, but not often. The chances are good that this is the last snow of this particular year-season. (Memo: If the person setting the New Year's date had been Canadian, New Year's would probably be June 1—July 1 in the High Arctic.)

Plows and shovels had pushed the last snow into banks, and the banks alone were left; all the snow on lawns and roofs had gone. The banks had pressed themselves into sheets of ice, under their own weight; then they'd half thawed and refrozen in the cycle of sun and cold. Now what stood by the roadside weren't piles of snow, but peaks and banks of collected ice crystals. Some banks were stained with the salt-sand mix the township puts down that

127

turns white snow into tobacco-colored slush, and the slush too had refrozen into turrets and ramparts of fine and magical ice—ice laced with small spaces where crystals had melted or sublimed into the fresh air. The sun glinted off white ice and brown ice with equal sparkling; neither the light nor the ice could know or care that some of these banks were still pure white and others were deeply stained. There was only the glittering beauty of ice and light.

The delicate constructions looked like some totally alien architecture. I wondered about fractals—the regularly irregular geometry of so much in this world that looks merely chaotic from a ninth-grade-geometry perspective. Fractal geometry describes the delicate, indescribably repeating lace of the outermost edge of a tide incoming. These ice shapes look fractal-like. Fractals are, to me, the place where mystery and mathematics kiss each other. I can barely manage senior algebra, so I don't understand this stuff. But I can imagine a chaos-theory mathematician looking at a snowbank like this and being knocked ass over teakettle by the sheer fractalness of it, the endlessly, mysteriously repeating figures, all this beauty in these shabby leftovers of a mild winter.

On the other hand, the practical Canadian side of me—the side that looks at an innocuously blank January sky with deep suspicion, because snow must be coming—knows that this beauty is as transient as a shadfly. The very light that makes the banks so lace-like and sparkling will also warm and melt them, and there will be no more piles like this until at least December, maybe January next year. We're already heading into Spring Mud Season, and then there's Spring itself, the only time of year when this plain beer-and-pretzels landscape actually rises to real prettiness. And then there's the bake of High Summer, the deeper, cooler half-melancholy loveliness of Late Summer, the great blare of Leaf Season, and the long quiet interlude of Fall Mud Season before we finally get back to familiar Winter—really the main season around here—with its shocking, piercingly blue dusks. But that's a long time off now.

So it's particularly important that I notice the snowbanks now, while they're still here. And it's particularly important—and particularly comforting to me—for me to train my hypersensitive senses on them, to see them with eyes that can't abide the sunlight, to lean down and touch their brittle fragility with skin that flinches shamefully at the slap of mere spring chill. I can only try to notice things, and if that means being able to use these uncomfortably heightened senses to notice them more sharply and more lovingly—well, that's still a hell of a lot better than simply being irritably hypersensitive.

Tomorrow may be a good day, a normal day, a day when my senses take a powder and chill out, and if it is, I'll be able to enjoy the March sun and the hints of spring—buds thickening, geese incoming in their great hopeful V's, hints of green in a roadside ditch. But the snowbanks, so full of beauty and mystery for a moment, will go back to being late-winter leftovers, like the litter left by the receding snow, black slicks of meltwater staining the road beside them. Good riddance!

If I can use my bouts of hypersensitivity to observe this poor battered graceful world more closely, then that redeems the hypersensitivity; it gives it a positive purpose. I'll have to find what means I can to do that with other symptoms, if I can.

*(Two days later it turned warm, and within hours the last of the snow was gone.)*

# ST. DISMUS AND THE TOADS

I can't find it in my big salmon-pink book of chil-
dren's stories, and I don't have any other likely sources around the
house. So I have to rely on long-ago memory to tell the old fairy
story; forgive me if I get bits of it wrong.

There is a nasty woman with two daughters, one nasty like her
mama and ugly to boot and one (inevitably) beautiful, good, and
persecuted. Mother sends good daughter out on some menial
task—I think it's getting water from the brook, something like
that. Good daughter encounters old woman who asks her help
with a particular task. Good daughter, naturally, helps old woman.
Old woman tunks good daughter on noggin with Magic Wand;

thereafter, whenever the girl opens her mouth to speak, rubies and pearls drop from her lips. Good daughter goes home, spitting gemstones all over the kitchen floor. Naturally curious about all these goodies, mother extracts tale of what has happened from good daughter.

Aha: if hated good child can have this gift, maybe beloved nasty ugly daughter can acquire it too, mother thinks. Next day, mother primes nasty ugly daughter and sends her whining down to the brook with a bucket. Nasty ugly daughter of course encounters the same old woman. Old woman asks nasty ugly daughter for help with the same particular task. Nasty ugly daughter fleers and jeers at old woman, refusing to help and ticking her off royally. Old woman tunks nasty ugly daughter with Magic Wand; thereafter, whenever the girl opens her mouth to speak, hideous toads and poisonous snakes drop from her lips.

I remember this story because sometimes I feel like the nasty ugly daughter: I open my mouth to speak and toads and poisonous snakes drop from my lips. This never used to happen, because in the Bad Old Days displays of anger always had to be paid for, immediately (of course), but also for weeks and months afterward. I learned better, I can tell you! But now that it's safe to get mad, sometimes I do. Something happens to bother me, and instead of walking away, raising a reasonable protest, or taking it in stride, or maybe bitching a bit, I suddenly find myself whirling in my tracks and heading smartly back to settle the score and give the offender a piece of my mind. I don't, thank God, do this to my kids, but my poor innocent bloke sometimes gets an ill-deserved snootful.

I call this behavior the Involuntary Snarlies. It *is* involuntary;

there is no premeditation, no volition involved. I can, with an enormous, exhausting effort of will, make myself *not* go back to settle
scores—but sometimes the Involuntary Snarlies sneak right past
me, before my conscious mind can take charge, and there I am
ready to wade in at high speed and be perfectly horrible. I can feel
the toads and poisonous snakes drop from my lips, and right then,
I'm not running the show. I can only stand by, dreading what's to
come and hoping I can set things to rights and pick up the pieces.

I hate the Involuntary Snarlies with all my heart, because they
make me feel so lousy about myself. I feel like a hateful person
when the ISs come upon me. I know I am hurting the person I'm
speaking to, and I can't stop myself. It scares me: *What price will I
have to pay for this later?* And I hate being so out of control. The ISs
invalidate all the household godlets I grew up with: self-discipline,
gentleness, patience, courtesy, consideration for others.

Anger is also one of the things a Christian can feel really truly
seriously guilty about—so much so that we often refuse to accept
that we *are* angry and try to cloak our rage in self-righteousness.
But my conscience won't let me do that, or not for long, thank
God. Instead, it shrieks and winces as I watch what the snakes and
toads—*my* snakes and toads, no excuses!—do to others.

Sometimes I feel alone with this problem, or I chalk it up to
my disorder. But then I talked to a couple of other people about
the Involuntary Snarlies, and it turns out that they're much more
common than I'd thought. Mind you, I should have known, having spent five years on an Internet mailing list, where the ISs oft-
times flourish. . . . Most of us do the same thing now and again,
saying things we'd never dreamed of saying, standing there appalled

as the toads plunk down on the floor before us and the snakes writhe into striking distance.

Sometimes, when you're on the receiving end of someone else's Involuntary Snarlies, you can see that these particular ISs are purely defensive. The person perceives a comment or statement as a piece of personal criticism (which it usually isn't) and flies into a toad-spitting rage, saying the most appalling things—and you can feel the defensiveness behind it, a deep unending ache behind all the fireworks. The person's words may sting a little, but they don't really hurt much. The snakes are just garter snakes and the toads are only ordinary toads, and neither has the power to do much harm. Defensive anger is too easy to see through. And it's too easy to see that the person doesn't have the confidence or security to say "sorry" or to own up to his or her defensiveness. That's just sad. It makes you wonder what the old damage was, and how deep it goes.

But others do much worse, and it doesn't seem to bother them at all. It doesn't seem to disturb them much when they say things that really do hurt or offend. They may feel perfectly justified in their nastiness (belligerently righteous: "I've got a right to say what I think, don't I?"). They may even enjoy biting others (exultantly smirking: "I got a really good one off at George!"). They seem completely untroubled by the damage they've caused, shrugging and walking away, or denying that they said anything hurtful at all (condescendingly: "You just can't take a little honesty!"). I've run into people with the habit of wrapping their toads and snakes in milk chocolate, so they themselves don't have to look at the ugliness dropping from their mouths (bewildered semi-innocence: "But I'm just telling you the truth in love!"). This seems to clear their consciences entirely. These are people I would much prefer not to hang out with, all things considered. I don't have to answer to God for them; they get to answer for themselves.

What I do have to answer for is the very real hurt my own words cause. These are *my* toads and snakes, and while I don't mean to let them fly, I have to acknowledge and accept the anger that creates and propels them—old anger, compressed and gray like very old ice; anger going back years, sometimes decades; anger that I couldn't acknowledge at the time, but stored away because at the time I couldn't see any other way of dealing with it. It's there. I have to accept its existence and try to manage it better.

But if this is the way I am, then I would much prefer to stand with the other people who sometimes say things that they desperately wish unsaid the moment they're uttered. At least they know how awful it feels.

This is the hard part: that I am sometimes going to have to eat those snakes and toads, a bitter snack. I am going to have to say to the other person, "I am so very sorry; I shouldn't have said that. It was unfair and unreasonable, and I know it was wrong. Please, if you can, forgive me; tell me what I can do to help you forgive." And I am going to have to say to God, "Have mercy on me, Lord, for I am a sinner—not one bit superior to all those other poor nebbishes I've been secretly despising all this time. And maybe I should thank you for reminding me of that."

I was thinking about this, and for some reason I remembered a church I'd seen in Kingston, Ontario, right near the walls of the Kingston Penitentiary, which is one of Canada's biggest, oldest, grimmest high-security penal institutions. The Kingston Pen goes back to the nineteenth century. In the 1880s prisoners were made to work on construction projects, some of them useful (building water towers) and some of them not (building walls, taking them down, and building them again). This church, built for the parish in which the Pen lies, was one of the useful projects. The prisoners built the stone walls and pillars, roofed the structure over, carved pews and woodwork—there were some fine craftsmen among them. The church was named the Church of the Good Thief. It's called St. Dismus, or sometimes just the Thief.

The prisoners weren't given any choice about building the church. I don't know if some of them simply resented the work, but perhaps others found a certain redemption in it. The Roman Catholics among them may have taken comfort from the fact that they were building a church—God might, perhaps, forgive them some of the past in exchange for this work. Perhaps a few of them prayed as they chiseled away, under the guards' bored gaze, at the fine pale gray limestone, cut on the prison grounds, and found some peace there. Maybe the fine woodworkers among them found some sense of reward, some comfort, in shaping pew ends and decorative moldings and screens. It was certainly better than building walls just for the sake of building walls.

I've never seen or heard of another Church of the Good Thief. But I think of St. Dismus when I get the Involuntary Snarlies. I don't come of a church tradition that venerates saints, but we do look at them with love, and that I can do for this Good Thief.

Dismus turns up in the Gospel of Luke. He'd been convicted of banditry fair and square and said as much to the other thief who was crucified with him and Christ. The other thief was mocking and railing at Jesus. Dismus told him to fear God's condemnation, adding, "We have been condemned justly, for we are getting what we deserve for our deeds, but this man has done nothing wrong." Here was a guy who was genuinely in the wrong, could accept that he was in the wrong, and still ask Christ to remember him in the kingdom.

Dismus, I think I need you to stand with me when I get the Involuntary Snarlies, and tell me the truth, as you told it to that other thief who was crucified with you and Jesus. I need you to help me acknowledge that those are real snakes and genuine toads. Please help me to accept responsibility for what I say. Those snakes and toads didn't ask to be tossed at another person; they're really perfectly innocent beings, poor critters; it's the use I've made of them that makes them truly ugly, not what they are in themselves. I have to learn to manage my own anger better, to see where it comes from and to try to prevent it from hurting others.

In all your guilt and physical agony, you could turn to the man on the cross next to you, who didn't deserve to be there as you knew you did, and you could ask him to remember you when he got into his own Kingdom. Dismus, good thief, tell me I can do the same.

# IN THE MOUTH OF THE LION

Maybe if there hadn't been so many triggers that week . . . but there had been. One good-sized one, an old piece of damage that I thought I'd long since gotten over (but I clearly hadn't), and a couple of other, smaller things, nothing I couldn't normally manage, but the good-sized trigger had already set me up, so that the smaller things pushed me a little further toward the edge. And then there was the newspaper story, and that sent me right over it.

The story was about an admirable man, a soldier who had served this country for thirty years. He'd been UN commander in Rwanda during the massacres in 1995. He had warned his superiors of the coming carnage and had urged a preemptive strike, but they had ignored the warnings and vetoed the proposed action. And when the massacres started, there was nothing he could do, except shelter those few who took refuge with his troops. Without overwhelming force, there was no stopping the killing, and he had only a thousand troops. He and his men stuck it out, refusing to turn their backs and leave, but effectively helpless, watching the atrocity unfold, suffering with the suffering. Now the horror haunts him in nightmares and uncontrollable flashbacks. He's had to resign his commission because his PTSD is disabling. If there's any healing for him, it hasn't yet begun. He'd been found that week collapsed in a public park, this man of huge courage and dignity and stoicism, curled up in a ball on the ground by a park bench. He'd been drinking. Who could blame him?

The article had that breathlessly helpful tone of the ambulance chaser who's covering up his or her emotional voyeurism with a veneer of concern. Clearly it was News, and equally clearly the journalist who wrote the piece had no real clue about what PTSD feels like. Not surprising. This is one of those things like childbirth or bungee-cord jumping; imagination gets you nowhere. You have to have *done* it. But in the newspaper article itself, and in the stock photo of his strong-boned haunted face that went with it, a scrap of his agony shone through, bright and clear.

And probably because of those previous triggers, that was that: I was off and running head down into the same bright agony, and once I was there, there was no turning back. I tried taking the appropriate pill and it worked enough to make me spacey and physically miserable, but it couldn't even begin to take the edge off the pain. This was spiritual stuff, and psychopharmacology has nothing to say to spirituality, or at least not that I know of. I knew that my secondhand suffering had nothing on his—as he probably feels that his suffering has nothing on that of the Tutsi victims. But suffering can (must?) be shared around. That's all we can do sometimes. I thought dully, as I leaned up against a wall while the pain sang and flashed: *Well, I guess the least I can do is to keep him company.*

Once it gets going, you are in the mouth of the lion, whipsawed: you are helpless and limp as a rag doll as the beast shakes you back and forth. The pain is clamorous and insistent, and it has its way with you. All you can do is try to control your own behavior: *I will not scream, I will not reach for oblivion, liquid or otherwise; I will not die, not yet.*

Meanwhile, the thoughts and images drift almost gently across your consciousness: notions of self-harm, of killing, of violent mutilations. They're strangely comforting, these images; they have a certain peculiar warmth; while they involve shockingly drastic acts, they have an aura of great calm and gentleness. I looked at the piece of art glass that stands in the window next to my desk, and imagined putting my fist through it, quite casually, and rubbing my wrist back and forth on the shardy edges. Things like that—you don't want to know. That day and most of the next week, tiny shocking images would float gently into, across, and out of my residually addled mind, like sparks across the eye's retina when you've squeezed your eyes tight shut for a minute.

And meanwhile life goes on . . . With enough practice, a person can drive herself and her two kids fifteen miles each way for hair-cuts, making the ordinary dumb family jokes, and then sit there for twenty minutes doing the standard small-talk-with-hairstylist even while she's having the emotional equivalent of a grand mal seizure. I've done this so often it's largely automatic now. I can find my way around the grocery store and chat quite normally with the cashier even while I'm doing a big-time flashback. At the same time, though, I could quite easily understand if someone else in the same emotional state were to flop down on the floor in the veg-etable department and throw a fantod. Eminently reasonable.

This time through, I stayed with it. I try as much as possible not to dissociate anymore; when I caught myself drifting away from the pain, I made myself go back to it. Dissociation is like any other addictive drug; you pay for the pain relief. But I did get some moments of detachment, the way you sometimes find your-self in a nightmare, standing off to one side and observing the fact that you're having a nightmare. They were like tiny breathers or the troughs between contractions. During one such moment I thought—I always do when the pain hits—of the people who have Real Bad PTSD (mine is merely middling) and who actually don't go nuts and kill themselves. Somehow they get through life, day after day after day. They have my deepest, most abject admiration. I want to walk up to them and fall at their feet, awed by their courage and fortitude. I want to kiss them. There are people who *live* with this. I just get the occasional fit.

And in another moment of detachment, I wondered if this is

what God goes through for us. I believe that God respects biology, physics, and human free will; God does not micromanage us
so that we don't get hurt or hurt others. The Rwandan massacre
was pure, unqualified old-fashioned human sin, perverted will at its
poisonous worst, and God has no more responsibility for it than I
do. But as that good man still suffers for the victims and as I suf-
fer for him, God is suffering for me—and for the general, and for
the victims, for the dead and the wounded and the survivors—and
also for their killers. God suffers powerfully and profoundly for all
who are damaged and all who have harmed them. God stands
there, loving us as we never manage to love each other, and God
weeps a whole lot, and our shards enter God's heart. And *we* think
God has to justify God's ways to *us???*

But then for the smallest fraction of a second, I saw something
else: that God's huge suffering for us is as a giant drop of ink
dripped into the vastest of oceans. Yes, God's suffering is immense,
but it dissolves so completely into God's joy that not an atom of
suffering remains. Not ink, now that I think of it; even in an
ocean, the ink molecules, however dispersed, remain unchanged.
More like matter hitting antimatter—except that the sum of God's
joy is not, even in the tiniest fraction, diminished by God's suffering. The suffering is real. But it is also obliterated. How this
can logically be, I don't know; but I've always been comforted by
the notion that my logic must be pretty crude compared to God's.

And also: God's time is not our time. Our time marches only
forward—that's the angel at the gate of Eden, Time—so that's all
we can see and imagine; but what if God's time can move back and

forth, like a bead on a string? Or even in three dimensions, like a bead in a box? Or in more dimensions than that? (This is where logic always lets me down.) Maybe C. S. Lewis was dead right when he wrote, shockingly, "This is what mortals misunderstand. They say, of some temporal suffering, 'No future bliss can make up for it,' not knowing that Heaven, once attained, will work backward and turn even that agony into glory."*

Some idiots might judge that good man for having been broken by trauma: "Hell, my dad survived four years as a Japanese POW and he was just fine!" But in fact it took courage and love not to duck out of the horror of Rwanda, physically or psychologically. He could have opted to leave. He could have opted to reject any understanding of the horror around him, instead of taking it inside himself. Ten thousand good officers would take that other course and might come out, if not unscathed, at least not so badly wounded. But that's not love: love looks like a clear-eyed child at reality, not ignoring or filtering out what hurts, but being willing to take others' suffering into its own heart. If he could do that for Rwanda, the very least I can do is to try to do that for him. At least a little. At least today.

There's the best of good company here in the lion's mouth. I am not the only one held and whipped around like this; you, God, are with me. I don't have to beg you to come down here and keep nigh me in this toothy, violent, shattering chaos, this hurl and hubbub, this sudden pit, those dangerous silences. You are here, re-deeming it all, taking it into yourself and transforming it into pure

*C. S. Lewis, *The Great Divorce* (London: Fount, 1977), p. 62.

gold. I may not be able to feel that redemption now, because I am still in the middle of it; inside a furnace, a person can't imagine the touch of cool and living water, but that's not because the water doesn't exist. The water is there, always.

May that good man, and I, and all others who know the lion's mouth, find that water, be soothed and comforted by it, and be made whole and happy and finally at peace, all in your own good time.

*Part Four*

# WRESTLING ANGELS

*Struggling in Real Time*

# IN EXILE

*These are the words of the letter that the prophet Jeremiah*
*sent from Jerusalem to the remaining elders among the exiles and to the*
*priests, the prophets, and all the people whom Nebuchadnezzar had*
*taken into exile from Jerusalem to Babylon. . . . It said: Thus says the*
*Lord of hosts, the God of Israel, to all the exiles whom I have sent into*
*exile from Jerusalem to Babylon: Build houses and live in them; plant*
*gardens and eat what they produce. Take wives and have sons and*
*daughters; take wives for your sons and give your daughters in marriage,*
*that they may bear sons and daughters and multiply there and do not*
*decrease. But seek the welfare of the city where I have sent you into ex-*

*ile, and pray to the Lord on its behalf, for in its welfare you will find your welfare. (Jeremiah 29:1–7)*

We moved downtown, because that's where he wanted to be: right in the center of the city. It was, at that point, an area full of 1930s apartment buildings in various stages of repair, the better ones full of civil-service mandarins' elderly widows in decorous hats and pearl-gray gloves. (Funny, almost thirty years later, the area is still full of the same widows, apparently unchanged. Are they immortal?) For three years we moved from one of these buildings to another, moving each time the rent went up because we were poor enough so that ten dollars a month made a difference. He was a student; I worked at various low-grade typing and clerical jobs, with a brief stint as cashier at a fish market. At that point, I had been seriously depressed for three years and had been told that this was a biochemical problem that I would have to live with for the rest of my life; I should consider not ever having children, as the condition was likely hereditary. Medication didn't do much. Mostly I just lived in the grayness—the gray of depression, the gray of the city.

On my way to work each morning, I crossed the big plaza at the center of the city, flanked by elaborate copper-roofed stone buildings. It was a sort of opening in the pressed-in feel of the neighboring streets, with their dense high-rise buildings. From there, you could see across the river, to the low forested hills beyond—hills much smaller than the mountains I'd grown up with and still longed for, but hills nonetheless: green in summer, gray-blue in winter, the right shape, the right color.

I wanted so badly to get there. But for two whole years we never set foot out of the city, because there was no public trans-port to the hills and we had no way to get there—and also be-cause, in my depression, I hadn't the strength and the will to do more than get through the absolute dead minimum of making a bare living and getting groceries. Oh, it was a gray time.

Exile is a gray state, a state of waiting, a state in which putting down new roots looks like much too much trouble, not worth do-ing. You'd had roots and they'd been ripped out; roots just get you hurt. You live in the hopeful expectation of getting home again, except that you can't see how you can get there this year, or next. You are Lot's wife, locked into salt and staring back at home. Where you are isn't where you ever thought you'd be, and it isn't what you want, either. Your children are straying from your cul-ture's ways; they're getting lippy, staying out with friends you don't know. You feel alienated by your poor command of the lan-guage, by your poverty and your foreignness. You face the quiet unacknowledged racism, day after day after day, the suspicion in people's faces and the cruel comments of bad children, and it saps the strength from your arms and legs like a bad flu that never ends. And you hate, really hate, the winters, which are terribly cold and seem to go on forever.

How is it possible to learn to love this gray place? How, in God's name, could you come to bless it and work for its welfare? It's like being torn from your true love's arms and given against your will to a stranger, and to a stranger who doesn't even know and like you—doesn't see a thing of your beauty and worth. How can you come to love where you are, when you passionately want to go home?

> *How could we sing the Lord's song in a foreign land?*
> *If I forget you, O Jerusalem, let my right hand wither!*
> *Let my tongue cling to the roof of my mouth, if I do not*
>    *remember you,*
> *if I do not set Jerusalem above my highest joy.*

But I know now, looking back, that the psalmist needed an attitude change and so did I. Jeremiah is right. You've always got the choice: to learn to love what you've been given or to make yourself miserable because it isn't what you wanted. That psalm starts so beautifully ("By the waters of Babylon—there we sat down and there we wept") and it ends in appalling vindictiveness: "O daughter Babylon, you devastator! Happy shall they be who pay you back for what you have done to us! Happy shall they be who take your little ones and dash them against the rock!" For that's where a person may easily fetch up: like Lot's wife, forever looking back, transfixed by what she'd lost, pickled in anger and longing as in a bitter brine, dreaming of vengeance.

It was wrong to stare at those mountains, wanting home instead of making home where I was. I turned my back on so much that the city might have offered, because it wasn't what I wanted—rather like sulking because you didn't get the Perfect Birthday Present, instead of enjoying the presents you had been given. I wish now that I'd looked around me more for joy than sorrow.

*T*here are exiles that have nothing to do with place at all. In my church, some Western dioceses ran residential schools for Aboriginal children during the 1930s through the 1960s. In these schools, there were dozens, perhaps hundreds, of cases of child abuse—physical, emotional, spiritual, and sexual. The accounts are horripilating. The church did little or nothing to protect the children from those who preyed on them. Now the schools' victims are bringing lawsuits, seeking damages for the horrors they'd been put through and the damage they'd suffered. The sums of money involved are huge—far more than the dioceses have. If the courts find against the dioceses, the dioceses will most likely be forced into bankruptcy.

What happens to a church that has to sell all its buildings, its properties, its organs, its liturgical vessels? If that happens, it will be a smaller, milder version of what the Jews went through when the Babylonians destroyed the Temple. Congregations will have to meet wherever they can. Will they be able to pay their priests? Will some churches simply go under—the congregations dissolving, because only the physical building had kept them going? The pain involved is going to be huge—although, in justice, so was the pain the children went through.

But while there's much anxiety, some church leaders are looking at this prospect with a strange serenity—almost a willingness to embrace the disaster. Maybe the church *needs* to do some wilderness time. Maybe it needs to be stripped down to a loincloth, a leather bag, a hat and a staff, and a blanket against the cold nights, and sent out to live in desert places for a while. Deserts have a way of purifying and strengthening the spirit; the air there is clearer and purer than it is in more comfortable places, and it is a place of great beauty, of strange fruits that you learn to look for.

I've seen others go into the wilderness for other reasons: a job loss, health problems, a divorce, the terrible loss of a child. Some of them have it so much tougher than I ever did; I don't know how they put one foot in front of another, how they get through a single day. I don't know. There may be situations so terrible that they'd simply break anyone who had to go through them. I've never been there. But I do watch people go into the wilderness and emerge from it transformed in ways that I could never have imagined.

I know the wilderness places, what you can make of them, if only you choose to look before you in patience and love instead of behind you in bitterness and longing.

*N*ow I live not in the city, but close to it—about half an hour's drive. I go there once a week or so for appointments or errands or shopping. It's changed some; it's now more variegated and more interesting, livelier and more attractive than it once was, and somewhat more friendly. But it is still recognizably the city I hated all those years ago. If it's changed some,

I've changed more. I'd still sooner be in the country, but if I had to move back, I think I could be happy there, or wherever I found myself planted.

The town I live in is no great shakes to look at, and the countryside is not beautiful, like the country I'd grown up in. It isn't, and can never be, my hometown. But I find plenty here to love: people who are quiet pilgrims, questing without fuss for a God whose love they know about; particular corners of the landscape; the quiet solidity of the river; the blue beauty of snow at twilight. I have indeed built a life here, not the life I ever expected, but one rich in small contentments. This is home now. It may not be home forever, of course. I don't know if I'll live out the rest of my life here or whether, when the kids are grown, I will pick up and move somewhere else.

Wherever we fetch up, if it's humanly possible (and I think it usually is), we are to "build houses and live in them, plant gardens and eat what they produce." We are to live wherever we are as fully and creatively as we possibly can, and we are to enrich and bless the places we find ourselves in, even if they aren't where we ever expected to be. It's peculiar how much more lovable even a plain place looks if you're prepared simply to love it, just as it is, without Pollyannaism or pretense. And it's peculiar how a place you've chosen to love can give you small daily gifts of pleasure and satisfaction. But this can happen only when you look at it with love, instead of holding it up against another landscape and telling it what a failure it is by comparison. No place, no person, no situation can stand up to that sort of treatment.

There is another home—I'd like to say "I believe," but this goes far beyond belief and into absolute gut faith—there is another home on the other side of the River; there's a place awaiting me that will be home forever, unlike any place on this earth, even the ones I love. And that home will be everything I ever wanted from a home, and then more than I can even begin to dream of. I get whiffs or glimpses of it every now and again. Part of me longs to get there just as soon as I can, but another part knows better: I am to live in *this* life, for the time being—and the time won't be forever. As Jeremiah goes on: "For thus says the Lord: Only when Babylon's seventy years are completed will I visit you, and I will fulfill to you my promise and bring you back to this place. For surely I know the plans I have for you, says the Lord, plans for your welfare and not for harm, to give you a future with hope." (29:10–11)

We are in exile from a life we've never yet experienced, and some of us know it and most of us probably don't. When the time comes, then I'll go home. But until then, knowing that my term here will have its natural limit sooner or later, I hope I can accept the world not as I want it to be, but as it is. That's not to say I'm off the hook: I do have a real responsibility to help change what needs changing, whether it's social injustice or the production of greenhouse gases. In the face of things that can be set right, it's wrong to flap your hands and say, "Oh, well, it's not a perfect world." If my house has carpenter ants, that's something I have to deal with. Mosquitoes, on the other hand, I just have to live with.

It *isn't* a perfect world; it's a wild mixture of joy and pain, of justice and hideous unfairness, of inexplicable beauty and equally inexplicable tragedy. That's just the way it is, always has been. The rain has been falling on the just and the unjust together for a very, very long time. To rail at this poor world because it isn't heaven is just as unproductive as staring back over your shoulder at what you've left behind you. We will all die, and some of us will die terrible deaths or die far too early. There will inevitably be floods, hurricanes, tornadoes, income tax, and the evil that stems from the wrongful exercise of human free will—not because God is ungood or unloving, but because this isn't heaven, it's earth, and it's silly to expect it to be anything else.

"Bloom where you're planted." It sounds like such a bromide, and sometimes it seems so impossible. But it's possible to find some richness in almost any soil, as long as you have the will; and the sun's the same wherever you are.

So don't look back; don't desire what life can't give you, at least not now. Build your house, unpack your boxes, settle down, explore the neighborhood, find people to love and be loved by, create whatever you're called to create, and trust that in the end you will be given Home.

# CAN'T CALL IT LOVE

*Beware of practicing your piety before others in order to be seen by them, for then you will have no reward from your Father in heaven. (Matthew 6:1)*

*The Portable Dorothy Parker,* like my old facsimile copy of that nineteenth-century English cookery classic *Beeton's Book of Household Management,* makes ideal bathroom reading, and so that's where my copy is kept. When Parker is intuitive about people, she can be terrific, and of course, like Oscar Wilde, she's one of the all-time Great Wits ("You can lead a horticulture but you can't make her think"). I also find some of her stuff self-centered and bathetic, but then, she was not a happy woman.

But sometimes Parker will write something that, underneath the surface sugarcoating, is the true salt of insight, like a deceptively sweet little quatrain entitled "For a Sad Lady":

> *And let her loves, when she is dead,*
> *Write this above her bones:*
> *"No more she lives to give us bread*
> *Who asked her only stones."**

Ouch. Bull's-eye!

This bugged me for years, because I couldn't evade the truth in it; it pinned me uncomfortably up against the wall. Or I kept running up against it, banging my shins painfully. Before life got so Interesting that I had no time or energy for such foolishness, I used to pride myself on being a generous, loving, caring person. I was always ready to lend a hand, always willing to drop what I was doing and help out; I spent hours listening; I gave out food and made casseroles for people and distributed loaves of bread left, right, and center. It felt good to do this. I could revel in being such a nurturing, earth-motherly, wise woman, concerned only for others. Being generous feels very, very nice.

But the Parker quatrain was like a thumbtack in my back

---

*Dorothy Parker, "For a Sad Lady," in *The Portable Dorothy Parker*, intro. by Brendan Gill (Penguin: New York, 1976), p. 88.

pocket. Every time I remembered it, my ego ached and I found myself thinking uncomfortable questions. What if my generosity was more a burden to others than a gift? I ruined one good friendship by racking up so many gift-points that the other person, who couldn't reciprocate, finally blew up at me in frustration and insecurity. In being endlessly helpful, I'd feasted my hungry ego without seeing how it starved her self-respect. In being "nurturing," I'd been reducing her to nursery status; in "helping" her deal with her own messes, I'd been carefully avoiding dealing with my own.

Which was particularly dumb of me, because I'd been on the receiving end of such generosity and I knew how maddening it can be. I remember the first Christmas the kids and I were on our own, and someone kindly brought me a food gift box—a grocery box full of canned staples. I think the assumption was that our pantry was bare and we needed, but were too proud to ask for, that kind of help. But in fact, we weren't poor. I didn't need food, and especially not food that my kids loathe and despise, like canned tuna. I suppose I should have been grateful; instead, I felt something about halfway between amusement and exasperation. Now, if someone had offered some help with the leaking garage . . . but nobody had asked what we needed. So I passed the carton along to the food bank (maybe someone loves el-cheapo no-name strawberry jam?) and hired a carpenter to tack plastic sheeting over the garage roof, to hold it until I could afford to get it properly fixed. Is this ingratitude? Probably. But it's hellish to feel obliged to be grateful for something you didn't want or need in the first place. I thought again of Parker's poem.

I thought of it yet again when I ran into a Sad Lady who did exactly what Parker wrote about—kept offering me over and over again the mushy loaf of Love when all I wanted was the good clean granite of friendly civility. I understood then an old paradox I'd never accepted before: rejected love often hurts the rejecter more than the rejectee. At least the rejected one isn't forced into choosing between being Mean and Unloving or having to choke down unwanted food. *(Gag!)* And being brokenhearted is far more socially acceptable than being a heartbreaker.

How can a good person reject love like this? Don't we all need and want to be loved? Don't we all secretly long to be nurtured and nourished? Don't we all hunger for that sweet and wholesome bread?

Not always. Think about it. You don't want a person to hand you a loaf of bread when you're trying to put together a camp fire-place. You don't want the gift of bread while you're making love, or when you just ate and aren't hungry, or when you're birthing a baby, or when you're passing a tractor-trailer on the road, or when you're in the middle of a really fascinating crossword puzzle. Except when the giver is a small child (children's gifts must always be received appreciatively, whatever they are), you probably don't want a loaf of store-bought white fluff when you have your mouth set for a good solid whole-wheat loaf. You may not want your neighbor's gift of that experimental zucchini-corn-and-jalapeño seven-grain loaf that didn't quite work out. Above all, you don't want bread when the unstated purpose of the gift is to put the giver one-up and you one-down—to establish the giver's spiritual superiority.

What's the difference between giving a starving man a stone when he's begged you for bread and giving a woman who's build-ing a wall a loaf of bread instead of the stone she asked you to pass her? Neither of these really considers the other person's needs. Neither really respects the other person's wishes. Often we think we know better for Jack than Jack knows for himself; isn't that arrogance instead of kindness? Or we think that Jill will just love this book because we just love this book and Jill must love what we love. Where's the Jill-person's reality in that assumption? Is it true kindness when the thought is kind but obviously hasn't done any real thinking? Is love really love when its expression pri-marily satisfies the giver's need to be (or be seen as) loving and giving—when it's scratching the ego's itch for admiration?

For that's what both the Parker poem and the passage from Matthew are about. The Sad Lady loves to see herself as giving: I can see her glancing with a small sideways smile at her image in the mirror, admiring the way her sleeve falls over her rounded white arm and the graceful turn of her wrist as she hands out a shapely loaf, while its recipient kneels in adoration to receive her generosity. A chunk of really useful rock just wouldn't look as nice. Besides, lifting rock is real work. But that's not love. That's pure vanity.

Ego and soul are in inverse proportion: the more we feed our need for our own or others' admiration, the less we do any real soul-building or growing, because we're too busy building a prop-erly handsome persona to give any real thought to who we really are. Of course we should take genuine pride in our achievements, remembering always that God gave us the wherewithal to work with. But handing out the wrong stuff, or the right stuff for the wrong reasons, isn't something to be proud of. It's like trying to teach a pig to sing: it's a waste of your time and it irritates the pig.

It's so easy to fall into the trap. We may or may not want real love, with its honesty and insight and terrifying real intimacy that sees us up close, exactly as we are. But not one of us doesn't like a little admiration. I've had to accept that I have an authorial ego, aged about two, who would much rather fatten on cream and honey than feed humbly on no-fat unsweetened yogurt. All I can do is admit that it's there, and insist that it doesn't get dessert until after it's finished its vegetables.

It's only human to want to feel and look good. It's even more human when, in your most secret places, you really need loving attention and praise and unconditional positive regard, and you are too scared and ashamed to admit how terribly needy you are. All of us are like that too, at least a little. In that sense, we all do need love.

But we need God's kind of love: a love stripped of all neediness and self-regard, a love that honors and respects us as well as nurturing us; a love full of thought and genuine care, that gives generously when that's what we need but that also gives us independence and freedom. God does not insist on doing what God most wants to do, which is what free will is all about, because God knows that controlling others or forcing them to be what you want and need is the exact opposite of love. God offers, but does not impose, Godself as a gift, for that is the deepest sort of courtesy. God's love does not burden us; instead, it leaves us feeling free, happy, respected for who we are, safe to ask for what we most want, and unafraid—ready to give our true, spontaneous, unforced thanks and praise. Now, that's the real bread, the whole-some loaf. I could use a slice or two of that. It doesn't need jam or even butter.

I shouldn't kvetch, I suppose. In a world that seems to be tum-bling deeper into selfishness by the day, any act of kindness, how-ever misplaced, should be worth something. Maybe if a misdirected gift doesn't do for me what the giver wanted, it does something to the giver that God wants done. I don't know. Maybe it's a sig-nal to me to be less selfish about what I need and more willing to accept whatever's on offer; true, I *need* that stone, but because it's a stretch for me, maybe it's more loving to accept the bread. Behind vanity, there's often a real need for reassurance; I know that in myself, and it's likely true for others. Besides, I've said before, and I will always say, that any gift given by a child, however poorly executed, is a treasure. Why do I have such trouble re-membering that we are all children?

# OF WOUNDS

It happened only last weekend: an ancient hurt that I thought had long since died and gone to heaven turned out to be very much alive. It shames me, sometimes, how things like this can hang on for years, entirely against my will. I want to be at peace with the person who inflicted the original injury, although she had never asked for that, or even acknowledged that she did anything wrong at all. But the knowledge of what she did lies between us, like a stone. She knows. She just doesn't want to admit anything. I want to forgive her so totally that the hurt never happened at all. I want to go back to the time before the hurt—to find the knot in this particular strand and patiently undo it. And it just doesn't happen.

I've wrestled this one for more years than I can remember, and the first, last, and only Law of Forgiveness that I can recommend with a quiet conscience goes thusly:

*Forgiveness is untidy.*

If you want your life to be neat, logical, and well regulated, may you never be given anything major to forgive. For forgiveness fol-lows no simple black-and-white laws—in fact, find me any simple black-and-white law governing forgiveness, and I'll find you a whopping awful case that proves that that law is a fool. "Always forgive" can turn you into a well-pounded doormat; are we never supposed to resist or oppose real evil? That's how (for example) domestic violence flourishes, or the oppression of any group by any other group. "Always remember" gets you Kosovo and Northern Ireland. No, I don't think so . . . "Beware of cheap forgiveness" is closer to the mark, but how does that fit with the Gospel? How, for that matter, does *anything* about forgiveness both fit with the Gospel and not rip the bejayzus out of natural justice and our own inevitable feelings?

Oh, the small stuff is (or should be) easy enough to let go of, especially if you keep in mind that most excellent adage: "Never ascribe to malice what can be adequately explained by stupidity." We're all supposed to be adults, and to be adult is to have devel-oped both a reasonably tough hide and the ability to laugh off another person's unintended piece of foot-in-mouth disease. Life is tough enough; if you're sensitive and easily bruised, it's going to make your life that much more difficult—all those peas under the thickest of mattresses . . .

But what about the big stuff? That's where forgiveness rapidly turns into a mess. Somebody sexually abuses my kids, and you expect me to forgive??? I don't think so. Somebody keeps doing the same damned thing over and over and over again because she's got a problem and won't admit it—am I supposed to forgive that or confront it? And then there's major Evil, the Hitlers and Pol Pots and Tim McVeighs: can any human soul do *that* work of forgiveness? And how can I forgive on someone else's behalf? *We* can't forgive Hitler; we can only record what he did. If there's any forgiveness possible, it has to come from his victims—and if they can't forgive him, who am I to tell them they're wrong?

Doesn't forgiveness at least require penitence first? And what if that penitence is fake? We all know the puppy-on-the-carpet sort of apology. Pup poops on parlor Persian. Pup looks at you with big brown Bambi eyes, wagging tail hopefully: "You're not *really* going to punish darling Me, are you? It was all a regrettable accident, and it won't happen again"—and of course it does happen again. The notion is to manipulate your victim to avoid the consequences of what you've done without really acknowledging that you've done anything much in the first place. Happens all the time: the utilitarian mea culpa that gives off a muffled, hollow "boom" when you thump it lightly with a knuckle, because there is nothing inside it but air.

But even when penitence is real and sincere, can it undo what was done? A person with paranoid schizophrenia shoots a man who he thinks has been persecuting him: the shooter is clearly mentally ill and not responsible for his actions. When his meds kick in, he is racked with grief and remorse about what he's done. He must actually be convinced that the crime is his illness's fault, not his own. Maybe the victim's widow can forgive him, but that doesn't alter the fact that her husband is dead. Forgiveness does not necessarily put everything to rights again. Forgiveness is not quite the same as reconciliation or healing, and reconciliation and healing are not always a matter of putting things back where they were in the first place.

It should be easy to forgive when someone's offered an apology. But when a person has done something truly unpardonably awful, it may so happen that that person isn't going to want forgiving. To accept forgiveness means that you understand and accept that you need to be forgiven, and that means that you recognize that you've behaved really badly. And that's very, very hard on the old ego. Easier to pretend nothing happened: "Mouse, what mouse? Do you see a mouse? I don't see a mouse." Hell is struggling to forgive someone who won't admit to having done anything wrong—who insists, in fact, on telling you that *you're* wrong ("You brought this on yourself" or "You should have gotten over this" or "Christians *have* to forgive").

I find it easy to forgive when the party of the second part is in "trouble, sorrow, need, sickness, or any other adversity." I was talking, the other day, to someone against whom I could hold a good solid well-founded grudge or three, and he's clearly so miserable on his own recognizances that anything foul I could do to him would be peanuts by comparison. When the enemy of your bosom is suffering from piles, shingles, periodontal disease, teenaged daughters with PMS, and an IRS audit, you can't rejoice over his ill fortune, not if you even pretend to be a Christian. After all, natural justice has had its pound of hamburger: your enemy did Bad Things to you and your enemy got blasted, just what the @#$% deserved. And so you can let go of your anger and your desire for revenge, because God has crushed your enemy like a bug, thank you, Lord. If anyone doesn't believe this is real, check out the psalms. What drives the psalmist screaming up the wall is not so much that his enemy has clobbered him as that *the bastard is going to get away with it.* "Where are you, God," he cries. "If you really loved me, you'd smite him cross-eyed!"

No: the problem is when someone has done you real and considerable harm of one sort or another; and the only sufferer seems to be yourself—when there is going to be no natural justice (no apology, no consequences, no plagues of locusts), and you can't find healing of your own. Don't tell me it shouldn't happen. It *does* happen. So what, for God's sweet sake, are we supposed to *do?*

Cheap forgiveness isn't the answer. Cheap forgiveness says: *Oh, it wasn't any big deal, and besides (s)he's such a nice person—I really should just let this go.* And yes, for small things, that's just the proper attitude. But not for the big hurts, the lasting ones, the ones that make you start crying in public places when you think of them. Cheap forgiveness is a Band-Aid—fine for little cut-finger wounds, but not for knife-in-the-gut damage. It is like wallpapering over re-ally bad plaster: one good prod, and it all falls apart. Cheap for-giveness springs to absolve the other, skipping all the necessary work: it skims over both the other person's very real wrongdoing and our own very real grief, hurt, and anger. Cheap forgiveness is scanting the soul-work needed for the genuine thing, because we'd much rather make nice than struggle with the truth.

For the truth is that without natural justice, forgiveness is go-ing to be bloody hard work; and the worse the natural justice im-balance, the harder the work it's going to be. Big natural injustice is the sort of thing that drives God-seeking people out into the wilderness, there to do forty laps, until they figure out what to do, or else give up and come back to civilization fervently hoping that God will figure the whole mess out and let them know.

And once you're out in the desert, it's just you and God, and nobody on God's green earth can do anything more for you than listen as you work out your own solutions. I don't know what hap-pened—and the facts of the case must always come first. I don't know what role you played in what happened, or whether you're as innocent (or as guilty) as you think you are. Perhaps you haven't paid attention to your own faults and the other's point of view—or perhaps you've let the other argue you into believing that it's your own fault and he or she just made a tiny boo-boo, when it really was a whopper. Perhaps what really happened is that the other guy inadvertently kicked an old sore spot of yours, and the degree of hurt was disproportionate to the kick itself—which does not, of course, diminish the fact that it still hurt like hell. Or perhaps the other guy was using that grand old passive-aggressive trick of going for your gut with the sweetest of smiles; it's so much easier to feed another person poison if it's nicely sugarcoated . . . Sometimes it's so bad that you go into shock and the hurt and damage don't emerge until much later. I said it was untidy. I just don't know. That's what friends and tea are there for: so that you can talk all this out, if you can.

Sometimes it is right to turn and embrace your enemy; sometimes it is right to refrain from embracing. Sometimes it's right to make the first step toward reconciliation. Sometimes it's wise to remember that those who refuse to acknowledge or understand the past are very apt to repeat it. Small forgivings may be as commonplace and uniform as Band-Aids, but each single act of big-time forgiveness is custom-built. And like anything custom-built, it's going to take time, effort, and a great deal of thoughtful work.

So why? After all, the world sees nothing much wrong with nourishing a good grudge; we're now encouraged and rewarded for baring our wounded souls, showing how cruel life's been to us. And there are acts that *must* be kept in memory, forever: the Holocaust comes to mind. The only natural justice we can offer those innocents is the justice of never, ever forgetting. Also, forgiveness does not actually *fix* anything or anyone: I may forgive my enemy, but what (s)he's done is apt to stay with me, like it or lump it.

But I do have choice: to head deeper into anger or to turn away and at least try to move Godward, and moving Godward is moving toward forgiving. I have to ask forgiveness too of those whom

I have wounded—because I'm no virginal innocent here; no one can live half a century in this life without doing at least a little harm to others. I have to both walk steadily through my particular desert of hurt and anger and aim to come out the other side of it. If I can't manage full reconciliation, maybe I can manage acceptance. Maybe, in God's good time, I can simply put whatever-it-is down and walk away from it.

I thought I had done that with that ancient hurt—the one all this started off with. Turned out, I hadn't. All I can think is that I'm still so imperfect at forgiving that I have to keep practicing, and that may mean going over and over the same ground until I finally understand. For the time being, back into the desert. Another forty laps: okay, if that's what you want, Lord.

# 1 CORINTHIANS 13:4-7

*Love is patient; love is kind; love is not envious or boast-*
*ful or arrogant or rude. It does not insist on its own way; it is not irri-*
*table or resentful; it does not rejoice in wrongdoing, but rejoices in the*
*truth. It bears all things, believes all things, hopes all things, endures*
*all things.*

Yeah. Sure. Been there, done that, for twenty-one years—the
whole core and center of my young adulthood—with a guy who
had Real Big Serious Anger Issues. But because he didn't want
to deal with these Real Big Serious Anger Issues, he gave them to
me to carry for him: *here; you hold this. I can't cope with it.* I got

to carry his anger for years. The result: I have a small-to-medium-sized case of post-traumatic stress disorder, and I will probably spend the rest of my time jumping half out of my skin whenever a door slams, getting mugged by flashbacks, and having breath-squeezing, throat-closing anxiety attacks which, I can assure you, are a pain in the keister, especially during choir practice.

One part of me says, don't give me "love forgives all, endures all." That kind of love—if that's what you want to call it—turns a person into a doormat, and that can't be what God had in mind for me or anyone else. Trying to fit myself into that particular mold was the dumbest damn thing I could ever have done. I've watched other people do the same thing, like Cinderella's stepsisters lopping toes and heels to jam their feet into the impossible slipper. I've seen people twist and squeeze themselves into ever-diminishing knots in order to fit into the "loving spouse" shoe, when it's quite clear to everyone but themselves that they're being used and abused like a bunch of suckers by spouses who take and take without giving—and deeply resent what little they do have to give. So don't give me 1 Corinthians 13. A recipe for disaster, if ever there was one.

But another part says: I still want those words back. I want to reclaim them, repossess them. I want to scoop them out of the thick black mud and pick the rotten bits of vegetation out from the centers of the *o*'s and the loops of the *e*'s. I want to wash the words clean with good fresh yellow soap and very hot water, and then polish them until they shine again and put them proudly in a place of honor. They're good words, words of great power and beauty. Is it their fault that I, and so very many others, mistook their application?

It's not a path you choose; you sort of slither down it without understanding where you're going. So many decisions are small day-to-day things that mount up, a few at a time, until all of a sudden they've taken on a life and direction of their own, without your ever really having made a conscious choice. Nobody chooses to stay stuck in an abusive marriage. It happens in such nickel-and-dime things that you don't really notice until it's too late, and then you're dug down so deep that getting out is no easy matter.

Scripture may be of God, but it was written down by people and was, is, always will be, interpreted by people. Paul says, a little later on, that he knows now that he only sees things imperfectly—think of a mirror with the silver reflective backing half worn off by the years, and the blurred images you'd see if you tried to look through that glass, mere shadows of reality. Only "then"— in the time to come—will we see God's love clearly, face to face, Paul says.

Until then, we're trying to walk the Kingdom way in this terribly confusing, imperfect world, mostly guessing at what God wants us to do and sometimes guessing wrong. Skywriting would be nice. But when I look upward, there's no trace of God's finger tracing out the words "Turn left here." I do the best I can. And sometimes I am wrong. I was absolutely catastrophically wrong in interpreting Paul's words as I did—but that's not the words' fault, or Paul's, for that matter.

The mistake wasn't trying to follow this particular set of directions. They're good directions. The mistake was assuming that I had no right to be on the receiving end myself—that I had no right to expect, as well as to give, all those good things, patience, tolerance, endurance, kindness, gentleness, all that I was expected to provide, unstinting. If there's no reciprocity, or too little, then something is very badly out of whack.

It didn't occur to me then (although it has, quite forcibly, since) that I was really trying to out-God God at the Being Good business—oh, the terrible subtlety of Pride!—when, in fact, the most truly loving thing I could have done would have been to look the guy sternly in the eye and say firmly, "STOP THAT RIGHT NOW, goddammit! Get help, or get out." And so it's not that I was perfectly loving—anything but. I was perfectly enabling (in the Alcoholics Anonymous sense), and enabling is not love. What kept me in that particular prison wasn't Love; it was Pride—Pride in what a loving person I thought I was being.

So if that wasn't love, what is?

I learned another time, and (again) the very hard way (observation: I seem to do this a lot), that love is not about Unconditional Positive Regard, because not one of us deserves that. None of us is perfect. If I ask you to look at me without seeing anything but sweetness and light, then I am demanding that you blind yourself to my reality for the sake of my egotism. I may choose to ignore my own failings, but I can't ask that of anyone else.

Love is also not necessarily all sweetness and light. I remember a friend translating the German adjective *gemütlich* as "niiiiizzze."

We think love will make things niiiiizzze; we think of ourselves as niiiiizzze, loving people. But love isn't always niiiiizzze; with the best will in the world, it can be messy and exquisitely painful, full of muddle and misunderstanding and conflicting needs and accidental injuries—and that's when two people really do love each other in the best sense of the word, eros and agape and caritas and all the other genuinely good things.

I learned from raising my children that human love is necessarily incomplete and deeply flawed. If there are any two people I know I genuinely love, it is these guys of mine; and yet I look back over our years together painfully aware that however much I loved them, I have also failed them in real and serious ways, time and time again. I can explain my failure, but I can't excuse it. I know they forgive me. I know that others feel the same about me—that they have loved me genuinely, but also failed me, and I have loved and failed others. The least I can do is forgive them, right? Because if we're going to be human and fallible, we're all going to need forgiveness. Anyone who thinks otherwise hasn't looked at him- or herself at all closely.

In love, we are such children, dressing up in Mommy's high heels and Daddy's hat, trying so hard to figure out what the grown-up world is like. We see some people like Mother Teresa or Jean Vanier or St. Francis who seem to be at least halfway there, and we wish we knew how to be more like them. But they'd be the first to say that they don't know either. Those who say they are loving, know what love is like, are probably further from it than those who say that they really don't have a clue and are just muddling through as best they can. The best that they or we do is somehow to allow the Godliness of all love to flow through, because it's all still of God however imperfectly we transmit it.

But oh—think of what it means if what Paul is describing is God's love—the pure type of love, of which our loves are such imperfect versions! Think of God's love as being as modest, as tender, as kind and patient and forgiving as Paul says. Think of falling into that love, of being held and surrounded by its extraordinary gentleness. It makes me think of Aunt Beast, in Madeleine L'Engle's *A Wrinkle in Time:* a gentle gray figure, apparently featureless and uninteresting, but with such healing tenderness in her touch that half-frozen, wounded Meg can relax back into her arms like a baby and be warmed and gently tended. Of course, that would be only one small aspect of God's love. On my good days, I can imagine other flavors and colors, facets of something too big and glorious for me to wrap my imagination around. . . . But for now, as I'm looking back at where I was, I think I still need that soft gray comfort.

So: hanging on to that image, I can lean back in God's arms, feel the warm body behind my body, and know that at least I did try to choose the right path, even if I got off on such a bad detour for a time. I can only keep on choosing love over the opposite— selfishness, indifference, unawareness, judgment, cruelty—because it's really the only possible choice, the only one with any outcome I'd ever want to live with. Yes, taking that choice will entail suffering: love and the willingness to endure suffering are one and the same thing. Nu? What else is new. It will be all right, for I will always have this warm comfort to return to. And in the end, I will indeed be able to see what Love is, in all its gentle glory.

There. The words are clean now; I give them a final rub with my sleeve and set them down to admire. A while ago, I sat in a gray limestone church down the street from my house, with a goodly number of friends and relations, and I sat hand in hand with a gentle man who does not have Big Serious Anger Issues, and we listened to these words being very well read, now that (for us both) they had been redeemed and made new again. Then we stood and made promises to each other in front of God and the congregation. And the greatest of these promises was love.

*Love never ends. But as for prophecies, they will come to an end; as for tongues, they will cease; as for knowledge, it will come to an end. For we know only in part, and we prophesy only in part; but when the complete comes, the partial will come to an end. When I was a child, I spoke like a child, I thought like a child, I reasoned like a child; when I became an adult, I put an end to childish ways. For now we see in a mirror, dimly, but then we will see face to face. Now I know only in part; then I will know fully, even as I have been fully known. And now faith, hope, and love abide, these three; and the greatest of these is love.*

# WRESTLING ANGELS

*Jacob was left alone; and a man wrestled with him until daybreak. When the man saw that he did not prevail against Jacob, he struck him on the hip socket; and Jacob's hip was put out of joint as he wrestled with him. Then he said, "Let me go, for the day is breaking." But Jacob said, "I will not let you go, unless you bless me." So he said to him, "What is your name?" And he said, "Jacob." Then the man said, "You shall no longer be called Jacob, but Israel, for you have striven with God and with humans, and have prevailed." Then Jacob said, "Please tell me your name." But he said, "Why is it that you ask my name?" And there he blessed him. (Genesis 32:24–29)*

You move into an old-fashioned small-town church slowly, a little at a time, because it takes a while for people to figure out whether or not you're someone they should take seriously. You can err badly by offering unasked-for advice, or by showing off, or by overeffusiveness—anything that gives people the impression that you're stuck-up, managerial, or intrusive. I have the natural disadvantage of a vocabulary full of three-syllable words, which inevitably (see?) dribble into the conversation. On the other hand, I can say "gidday" just like a native, and I understand gentle small-town teasing. More important, I do understand the rules. What might feel like initial coldness and caution is just something you have to weather in the expectation that if you're patient and stand there long enough, sooner or later someone will come over and talk to you. Maybe this isn't the way it ought to be, but it's the way it was when, all those years ago, I started back to church. (Said church has changed a lot since then and is now a very welcoming place.)

I came back for the same reason that most people come back after a long absence from church: I had young children, and I wanted them to have a church upbringing. More than that: my kids had little enough exposure to my side of the family, and I wanted them to have a little of what I'd had at my home parish, St. Pete's. (The latter proved to be impossible, for all sorts of reasons, but by the time I figured that out, it was too late.) Also, I was new in town, and church is a good place to start finding your feet in a small town.

What I didn't figure into the decision was any notion of real faith. By that time, I'd been away from Religion for the best part of twenty years. In general terms that I'd never much thought about, I supposed that God existed, and I had no serious quarrels with the basics of Christianity. But it wasn't a big deal to me, and I couldn't imagine it becoming so.

I'd had a promising childhood, full of what I now see as being richly Godful places and occasions; I had been as comfortable with the world of the Spirit as a child running barefoot across her own backyard. But when I went to college, the prevailing culture shamed me out of "that religious shit." I succumbed to its gentle, amused contempt and turned my back on "childish things"—disastrously, as it turns out, but that's another story.

In the fullness of time, I'd actually come to agree with the opposition: I rather looked down on Christians who took "that religious shit" too seriously. I wanted a detached, rational, elegant eighteenth-century sort of Anglicanism, not what a detached, rational, elegant eighteenth-century Anglican would have called (with deep suspicion) "enthusiastic religion." That, to my mind, was naive and self-serving and in not very good taste. My own approach to Religion, I decided, would be dry and light, a little distant.

It never ceases to amaze and delight me that our God is indeed a sneaky bastard.

I remember, a couple of months after I'd started back to church, the first spiritual moment I'd had in years and years. And it was pure panic. I saw myself standing in a gully, a sunbaked place of pure clean rocks, very clear-edged and simple, very quiet, and very,

very dry. From where I stood, I could hear in the distance (but not far enough in the distance!) the roar of water. I foresaw myself swamped, picked up and tumbled ass over teakettle, bashed and ravished by a flash flood of God. And I prayed—truly prayed, with all my heart, the first real prayer I can remember making, a sinful and treasonous and cowardly prayer that I couldn't help praying, knowing how wrong it was nonetheless: "Please, God, *please* don't give me anything more than I can handle. I can't handle a torrent of faith. Please, God, only a trickle."

And in response, that quiet neither-a-voice-nor-a-feeling-but-both, very deep and quiet: *Okay. I understand. Don't be afraid.*

It's only looking back that I can see that grace came into my life not bowling me over with a great knock-you-off-your-donkey Conversion Experience, but slowly and with great gentleness: not an exhilarating surge of sudden flood, but groundwater seeping up gently, unnoticeably, little by little making the sere land green again. Given where and who I was at the time, it's the only way I could possibly have accepted God. Years later, I learned the concept of "grace prevenient"—grace walking before you, but unnoticeably, preparing your way, making the path smooth before you. The unknown, unnoticed God who moves imperceptibly. Something like that.

It was natural, then, to slip deeper and deeper into parish life: to join the choir, to become a member of the parish council, to start to take root in my church community. It was not entirely a happy or easy process. The parish was a difficult sort of place at that time, full of divisions and tensions between groups—tensions that erupted after a few years, costing us a painful number of people.

But then, when the dust died down, the church seemed to be doing better. It looked like we were turning around. I found myself in the midst of a new circle of friendship, one where (for the first time in my adult life) I felt genuinely part of the community, welcome and valued. Little by little I shifted my emotional life over to this group. It seemed like such a safe place, a refuge from my strained and sometimes violent marriage, a substitute for the family from which I had to keep my distance. And in this safety, I started to unpack the past—to examine my early twenties and make sense of what had happened, to heal and to forgive, and to start to emerge as a vulnerable and very shaky soul. I think maybe that if that sense of refuge had lasted, I might have found the strength to acknowledge that my marriage was no good and to put an end to it. But that's hindsight; who knows?

But it didn't last. It all went wrong, with a Godalmighty bang that left me reeling. The details don't matter. Mostly it was a muddle of misunderstandings and miscommunications, of irritants that had built up and needed to be discharged but were discharged badly. Much (but not most) of it was my own fault. But still there it was: my sense of trust and community blown sky-high in a single afternoon . . . I caught a major blast from someone I loved dearly. That was bad enough; but there was worse: I learned of a piece of betrayal by a close friend, someone whom I'd trusted far more than I should have. Sirach nailed it neatly: "Love your friend and keep faith with him; but if you betray his secrets, do not follow after him . . . for he is too far off, and has escaped like a gazelle from a snare" (Sirach 27:17, 20). That was the worst of it.

I can look back now and see why my emotional responses were so overwhelming, but at the time, I didn't understand a thing. I was stunned by the intensity of my reactions; I felt they were to, tally out of proportion, but to my shame, I couldn't stop them. I am extremely good at handling emotional pain—lots of practice!— but this went on for weeks, then for months.

I remember being paralyzed with what I now see as depression: I'd sit on the sofa, unable to move for hours. And typically, I had no way of coping but to withdraw into myself, trying not to show anything of how I felt, and probably confusing the hell out of everyone around me. It was only long after the fact that I really understood what had been going on—the other factors that I hadn't been aware of at the time. We never do really understand the swamps we're in, only the ones we've left behind. That's the way it is.

The fact that I couldn't straighten things out bothered me very badly. I knew what my own part in the problems had been, and I felt so overwhelmed with guilt and shame that I couldn't speak at all, and the others involved had decided that "let's put this behind us and move on" was the best approach. I couldn't untangle the mess with my former friend either, because she is a person who never, ever does anything really wrong. She will cheerfully admit to making the occasional bitty mistake, but never to a real whop, per—that's just the way she is. Yet I felt whoppered. If I tried to explain how I felt, I knew from my knowledge of her that I'd be handed all the wrongfulness of the situation to carry, and I could not bring myself to do that. (Indeed, years later, when I gave her the opportunity, she obligingly did exactly what I'd expected. Nice to know I'd got it right.)

There I was, firmly stuck, spinning my wheels, caught between the need to forgive and a sense of such grief and anger that I couldn't forgive. But I had to forgive. But I couldn't forgive. And so round and round and round we went.

That was the moment I first wrestled with angels.

*A* sidebar on angel-wrestling:

Angel-wrestling is the hardest work in the world, not excluding childbirth; and that's when it's going well. It takes a real dug-in stubbornness to tackle angels. I once met what I'm pretty sure were Real Angels (actually, there were four of them—it's a long story), and I can assure you that they are impressive. The popular images have it all wrong. Angels aren't fluffy or cute; angels do not have nice little Renaissance wings, nor are they chubby little boys with dimply backsides. Angels are *big* muthas. The ones I encountered had a sort of coppery massiveness and seemed to be of an almost unimaginable denseness and solidity. Angels are huge and dangerous creatures, solid as pillars, unbudgeable. They may be protective, but they also test you. You can't really win, wrestling with angels, and you may find yourself with a dislocated hip, as Jacob did.

But there's also exhilaration when you get hold of that massive smoothly coppery form, digging your feet into the soil, bracing yourself against the weight, and thinking calmly: *Okay, how can I use a little leverage here?* I don't understand extreme sports; I cannot, for the life of me, fathom the exhilaration and joy some people report when they (say) jump off large freestanding objects. But angel-wrestling—now, *that's* a charge.

*T*hat's what I figured out later. But for the time being, there I was sitting pinned on the sofa like a moth on a collector's pin, completely immobilized by this whole forgiveness thing.

*Jesus said, if you don't forgive, you can't expect to be forgiven.*

*I don't seem to be able to let this hurt go or get over it. That's not forgiving. That means I'm definitely in the wrong here.*

*My former friend wants to make like nothing happened. I just can't do that.*

*What is forgiveness, anyway?*

It took me the best part of two years of the hardest angel-wrestling I have ever done—and even then, I had to leave that church for a while. (I'm back there now.) I had a number of things to learn, and I had to learn them the extremely long and hard way, testing them out, doubting and discarding, picking up and reconsidering the discards. But the process . . . ah, the process . . .

I got completely stopped by the theology of forgiveness. What does it mean, to forgive? I have never in my life been able to read formal theology; when I try even the best-written stuff, my eyes slide slowly off the page, like a car sliding over wet glare ice into the ditch. I can't help it. But I am lucky in having a mother who is, in her right, quite a good theologian and who loves formal theology the way I love playing FreeCell. We talked a lot. I kept sliding off in one direction or another; she kept bringing me back. In the process, we rebuilt our relationship, but that's another story.

The first thing I had to realize was that when I looked at my ex-friend and saw her problem with honesty, I was guilty of the same failing. *If you see a louse in someone else's hair, first check your own scalp for nits of the same species.* Well, there were nits of the same species on my scalp, and so I had to unlearn my need for *gemütlich* niceness. I had to develop a sense that strict truthfulness with oneself is an extremely important duty—one we never quite manage, but at least we should try. That was a step. Angel scores one: the notion of integrity. If the talk matters, the walk should follow it.

*Very nice,* says the Angel. *I'm glad to see you have a logical mind. You're cute when you're being cognitive.*

WHOMP. I'm down in the dust, scrambling up again.

Discovery 2: I am not God. I am human and God is God, but God isn't human, although he knows how it feels, having been there, done that. I can't imagine what God's forgiveness is like, except that I'm certain that, in it, love and insight are the same thing. We will have (in Dorothy Sayers's wonderful phrase) to "find the courage to look our hearts in the face," seeing ourselves with a full clarity that we can never reach in this life—but we'll be held lovingly in God's hand, supported and tenderly cared for in the process. We will be forgiven, but we will also understand what we are being forgiven for. Sometimes that will feel very much like hell. But if we're willing to go through it, instead of fleeing God's clarity, we have so much love to look forward to. My forgiveness is not the same as God's. What matters is that we work at forgiving—that we point our noses in that direction and keep trying. Forgiveness isn't an action, it's a process. It must be worked at and can't be forced.

*The Angel doesn't even bother answering this one. He's got me in a half nelson, and I am scrabbling at his forearm and trying to kick him in the shins. But he's too big; I can't reach.*

Discovery 3: Forgiveness isn't wiping the slate clean, as though nothing had happened. That's dishonesty and reality denial. For starters, "those who don't remember history are condemned to repeat it." Also, our actions have their impact on others; if we try to pretend that nothing happened, the other guy is left holding the bag for our behavior. My friend had been requesting cheap forgiveness, the type that pretends that nothing *really* wrong had happened: "Mouse? What mouse? Do you see a mouse? I don't see a mouse." I can choose (and I hope I do choose) to overlook any number of unimportant mice. But that doesn't mean they don't exist. I may choose to say, "It's okay; I know you didn't mean to break that plate-glass window, and I'll pay for fixing it." But you don't have the right to say, "Oh, well, I didn't mean to break that window, so it's not my fault. Christians are supposed to forgive.

Have a nice time fixing the window. I know it's expensive, but you can afford it."

*You think you know the first, smallest thing about justice?* growls the Angel, picking me up off my feet and squeezing so hard I feel my ribs starting to go. This isn't getting us anywhere.

Discovery 4: Forgiveness isn't necessarily reconciliation. I could, in time, forgive my false friend; that doesn't mean I want to be her friend again. Forgiveness is letting go of the pain and anger you feel and being free of resentment toward the other person. Reconciliation demands more than forgiveness. To be reconciled, you have to have the issues out on the table and dealt with. Thinking about this, I realized the deep truth of the pattern of our new Eucharistic liturgy: we have, closely linked, confession, absolution, and the exchange of the peace. If I have hurt you, I need to acknowledge the problem. It's your job to tender forgiveness and mine to accept it; then we can reach out for that reconciling hug. Problem is, people often want to skip one of those steps. That is, they don't want to acknowledge that they did anything wrong (and being forgiven is a blow to the ego, because it acknowledges that wrong did happen), or they don't want to let go of a perfectly good grievance. Either of those blocks true reconciliation.

*Ohfergawdsakes!* Angel bellows. *Aren't you ever going to get it? You haven't forgiven her. You haven't even started to forgive her. You're just running around in self-justifying circles trying to argue forgiveness away. I am going to have to get tough with you, you miserable excuse for a Christian.*

OWWWW. There goes the hip, ripped from its socket for

one blinding second before it pops back in with a revolting crunch. I am in excruciating pain. I am down in the dust, now, flat on my back, writhing in such pain as I've never known before, pinned by Angel's massive weight: ten, nine, eight, seven, six, five, four . . . Angel's face is in my face now; now there is no way out.

Angel, dear Angel, I am a SINNER. I am not just a nice person who sometimes makes an itty-bitty error of judgment; not me. Me, I miss the mark, big-time. I am quite capable of being bitter and unforgiving and judgmental and generally all those things that our Lord and Savior bopped those poor Pharisees for. I am not, in fact, always very good at forgiving when I should forgive—just as I am not always very good at confronting when I should confront. And I am often completely lacking in the wisdom to know the difference. The hell with what my friend had done. My failure was *my* failure, and that was the thing I was supposed to be working on.

*Well,* says Angel, standing up and helping me to my feet just as the first red of dawn streaks over the creek, glinting through the bare treetops. *Took you long enough.*

I dust myself off, feeling strangely light, although my hip hurts like hell. For the first time, I really *know* that it is okay not to be perfect. This time I'd really tried, tried as hard as I could, and I'd failed. At least I *knew* that I had failed. And suddenly, there I am, standing with the tax collector over in the corner, appalled by my own failure, and so relieved to feel God with the two of us there. He looks at me and I look at him, and we both start to laugh and hug each other. The hell with that guy in the perfect white robe, looking at us with such contempt. I am giddy with the happiness of knowing what a wretch I truly am. *Saints know what God wants. I don't know what God wants. I think I'll stick with the sinners.*

Angel blessed me, embracing me with arms now strong and gentle, and departed away from me. My hip ached for a while, but then I got over it, went back to church, and picked up the strands again. My former friend and I are on cordial but not close terms. We smile at each other and ask after each other's children. Civility will do, very nicely.

Other angels have since come to the wrestling floor at Peniel, and we have locked arms, dug in our bare toes, and struggled through the night, although no angel since the first one has felt the need to dislocate my hip. The first one taught me the knack of wrestling, and that's the hardest part of the learning. Now I look forward to these nighttime bouts. I've never won one yet, and I don't expect to—if you think you can, you've never met a wrestling angel yet!—but losing a match with an angel is greater than winning a match with even the greatest of mortals.

Come on, angels; I'm out here waiting, and it's getting dark.